Ancient Wisdom. Modern Minds

Demystifying the Spiritual Process

By C. (Tripp) Maxwell

FORWARD

The purpose of this book is to help people understand eastern spiritual practices in a way that makes sense and allows them to progress on their path. Eastern spiritual practices started in Asia thousands of years ago and were written in a language that isn't in current use except for religious studies. Supposedly there is a village in India where Sanskrit as their first language is still used. Sure, more scriptures and books were written in more modern language, but even those seem cryptic to us. You must also consider the eras and cultures they came from. The Indian texts used a lot of stories to pass along ideas. Whether or not those stories were literally true or figurative is up to debate as there are those who believe each side of that possibility.

There's also the way that the brains were formatted in the people who lived during those times. To those of us in the modern western countries, a dream is just a dream. And we've used science to essentially brush aside our dreams as random, mundane activities of the brain. But to people thousands of years ago a dream was very mystical and they paid attention to them. So in order to understand any ancient spiritual text, whether or not it is Buddhist, Christian or other texts a person needs to know a good bit about the culture of those people in those eras as well as linguistic understanding of how they spoke. Even in our lives we use phrases that a thousand years from now will make little to no sense.

Especially if future archaeologists attempt to decipher the copious amount of acronyms we use to shorten our conversations.

This book is not a belief system. It is a toolbox to allow you to explore your own experience in this creation we call life. It can help you search for the truth and doesn't demand that you believe it. If you are willing to put in effort to experience this life it will reward you with all sorts of understanding, wisdom and compassion. Try to empty your mind of all expectations and concepts of what you think will happen. These will only hold you back.

The way I have written this book isn't based on what would be considered normal writing standards. I write it in a way that I feel will help you understand concepts in a more efficient manner. If you are an English major and find the writing to be offensive then your own mind is going to block you from understanding what is written as you will only focus on what you feel is wrong with the writing. In other words you will be looking at the finger that is pointing at the moon and criticize it's posture while missing the splendor of the moon itself.

This book will have two main parts. The first part is the education and practices necessary to get your mind to flip perspectives, known as awakening. The second part is for what comes after that.

SPIRITUAL CANDY

In today's society we have access to a near unlimited amount of information. Yet we swim in a wasteland of useless information. The same can be seen in the spiritual community. People look for the newest fads and anything that pops or attracts their minds. They get hung up in the mystical arts of spirituality not realizing that they are just tools to be used to enhance our health and lives. Everywhere you look you will find singing bowl classes and certifications, Reiki and other old and new healing systems, tuning fork therapy, hot yoga, and on and on. This isn't spiritual. Someone out there is going to send me hate mail because of this. And that's fine.

As you progress in this book you will learn about the mind and the software inside our brains we call ego. Ego loves big flashy spectacles and events. It searches for the mystical stuff that it believes is going to make it more "spiritual". But all of the big flashy "spiritual" stuff that you see flooding the internet only feed the ego. Therapies are used to treat symptoms. Much like how massage therapy is used to treat sore and cramped muscles and release tension. But if you don't understand how the core spiritual practices of eastern spirituality work then you are not getting to the root of the problem. You can go to as many singing bowl classes as you want, attend as many gatherings as you want, buy as many crystals as you want. But if you don't know how to keep your own mind in check you will not get rid of whatever depression or anxiety, trauma or regret that may be living in you or you won't be able to experience the deep levels of a truly spiritual life that often comes in very subtle ways.

People are starting to see this. All of the big flashy "spiritual candy" is now giving people belly aches. They are realizing it's not getting them where they really want to go. Which is actual internal peace, connection with the source of creation, or getting further down the path of spiritual enlightenment. And now I am seeing an influx of true seekers. People who recognize that all of the fluff they've gotten into hasn't solved any of their issues and isn't doing anything other than giving them a quick fix of dopamine.

There will be those that read these words and their ego will jump in, get upset and then attack me for saying them. And they won't read any further as they just want to do what their ego wants them to do. Then there will be those that see that there's truth in these words. Sure the truth will sting, but they will feel a pull deep within to continue seeking the truth in life. These are the people I wrote this book for. Not everyone is ready. The old quote "For those with eyes to see and ears to hear" holds true in this book.

JUDGMENT VERSUS OBSERVATIONS:

Some people that call themselves "spiritual" build up an enormous wall of defenses in order to maintain their belief structures. And one of the most common phrases that is used as a weapon is "You're not very spiritual if you are judging people". There's a difference between judgment and observation. A judgment is when you think of yourself as better or other people as lower than you. Where there's a negative connotation to what you are saying about someone. An observation is just an observation.

In life there are ways that are more efficient than other ways. It's easier to cut a loaf of bread with a knife than with a hammer. If you were to see someone trying to cut a loaf of bread with a hammer you may think that the action the person is taking is not an intelligent action if they are trying to achieve a cleanly sliced piece of bread. But the moment you say something to the person and they say "stop judging people" then you realize the person just needs to go through their own trial and error in life.

The mental defense that some people use to defend their beliefs is just a big layer of ego. There's no real judgment there. It's just that they choose not to see truth as it is. They want to believe a certain something. And nothing you say will ever convince them otherwise. Read any literature written by any spiritual teacher, including the modern ones, and you will find them talking about their observations of the way people do things in a foolish manner. Or a manner that may not be very effective or foolish. This is one of the reasons why people in monasteries don't really get into arguments with people about anything. They recognize that the person is just defending a belief and doesn't want to hear any information that contradicts that belief.

And judgments do have a use in life. If a pipe breaks in your house and you need a plumber, do you just pick up the phone and call the first number you see? Most people tend to look for reviews of companies and people to see if the customers were happy with the results. In this way you are essentially passing judgment on a person you've never met based on their performance.

Same thing can be said about a person that you know likes to get drunk and fight. Every time this person gets invited to a social gathering they get highly intoxicated and get into fights or break stuff. It's not unreasonable for people to not want to invite this person to social events based on their behavior. Sure we can try and help them get over their drinking issues but only if they will accept help. Until then it's okay to love from a distance. So, if a person says they don't have ANY judgment, they aren't being very honest.

PART 1

SETTING THE FRAMEWORK

SPIRITUAL ABC'S

If you think about the spiritual path like the alphabet, or an encyclopedia then you can imagine it in terms of A, B, C, D all the way to Z. If we consider A the beginning of the path and Z to be ascension (turning into pure energy and going into another dimension), then we have a path that we can follow. As long as there are no deviations and everything happens perfectly. But life often doesn't move in a perfect straight line like we want it to. It's possible that a person has a grand mystical experience that opens them up to other amazing experiences. But big mystical amazing experiences without any foundation can be dangerous. A person can gain a messiah complex, start a cult, believe they are superior to other people, chase mystical practices without a basis of self understanding which can lead to other problems, etc. That's why in monasteries they have a regular practice and people who have come before the students in order to guide them away from pitfalls and traps that can cause serious problems.

Many people in modern western countries are drawn to mysticism and powers but avoid the deep inner work that requires discipline and dedication. As you read further and begin to grasp the concepts you will understand the "why" people are doing these things. It's easier to find a Yoga studio with drums and singing bowls than it is to find a truly wise teacher teaching a genuine path that understands ego and the esoteric teachings.

I'm not saying that there's anything wrong with singing bowls or different kinds of practices. But they are not a direct path to deeper understanding. They are tools and have a purpose. But people become fascinated with the toys in this world and get sidetracked from the amazing revelations that come from truly deep understanding. If you look at the lives of the past enlightened masters such as Yogananda, Lahiri Mahasaya, Layman Pang, Rumi, etc. you will not see hardly any of our modern day spiritual fads being used. Even the big name modern spiritual teachers. These masters were / are deep by themselves. They didn't need anything outside of themselves to reach these deep states. Sure, tools like singing bowls can aid in reaching deep states of consciousness while meditating. That's what they were used for. But there's so much commercialized spiritual fluff in modern western countries that it makes finding the genuinely deep teachers harder.

An amazing lady that I recently met and spoke to prior to writing this book is a truly deep individual who practices Ashtanga Yoga. After speaking with her for a good bit of time I saw the depth of her understanding. And I made the comment that I had never met a person in any of the Hatha style Yogas who had that level of spiritual understanding. She said that often people would come to her studio and if she didn't have drums and bowls they would leave. They weren't interested in the deep teachings that she had learned from her mentor. How sad that people are so sucked into these spiritual fads that they can bypass a true gem such as this amazingly deep Yogini (female yoga practitioner).

COMMONALITIES:

All eastern spiritual practices share a common starting point. The ancient Rishis of India. These mystics and sages used a scientific approach to exploring our reality and different states of consciousness and they recorded them. You can find their teachings in the Upanishads and the Bagavid Gita as well as other various works. After Gautama Buddha's life many books were written. And the Buddhist monks over the years wrote many, many more books detailing their experiences and practices. But because we all share the same reality people from all over the world discovered the same findings even if their cultures had never crossed paths. Hawaiian Huna (their form of spiritual practice) shares many similar discoveries and practices as Yoga. You'll find similar ideas in Native American spiritual practices. What this means is that our reality shares common traits that anyone can explore. We consider these to be universal truths.

ENLIGHTENMENT:

This term is extremely overused, misunderstood, and has had it's goal posts moved many times to suit those who keep the information. Sometimes information is withheld in order to keep people paying money or tribute to the master or monastery. To call oneself "enlightened" is silly and you will not find genuine people refer to themselves as enlightened. But they will talk about it in order to help other people. And the reason is because enlightenment as an object or a goal doesn't really exist in the typical way that people think. In martial arts a person may receive a title of "master" but if you talk to them they will tell you that they are still learning. This is truth. You will always be learning, as long as you don't resign yourself to your belief structures. But...........I will attempt to give some basic information as to what "enlightenment" is in order to better help people.

The first part is the realization of the mind and what it does to you. How it controls you and causes pain. Not to just yourself but to others you interact with. This first part is not easy to achieve as your mind will play games in order to keep you in it's control There are people who practice spiritual lineages for years and never achieve this. Some spiritual teachings are better at teaching certain concepts than others. Zen does a really good job at helping people achieve this first part. But I have seen people achieve this in easier ways.

The second part is staying free of the mind so that you can directly experience our reality without preconceived biases. This is where a lot of deep understanding comes one after the other, usually in rapid succession.

The third part is becoming centered and balanced and relaxed in this understanding of yourself and this reality we live in. A person in this phase lives in a flow state and is a truly blessed individual. Everything they need seems to be provided exactly when they need it. They also affect others around them in positive ways. The deeper this person's connection to the source of our reality the more miraculous events that happen around them. Some of these people are considered saints due to the way reality seems to move around them. And saints are not limited to the eastern practices and Catholicism. There are always stories around the world of people who moved this way in life.

Final thoughts on this horrible concept of enlightenment. Many people will say that enlightenment can't be described. And that those who describe it don't actually know what it is. Part of this is true. Once a person gets past the mind's influence on their reality around them then they begin to experience things that don't make sense to the logical mind. Many of these experiences really can't be put into words in a way that makes sense (I will go into more details about this later in the book). And so with that part I agree with. What I don't agree with in regards to people saying enlightenment can't be described is the mental and physical aspects that absolutely can be described.

Unfortunately the cultures of the east combined with mystical sounding texts on top of dogmatic approaches has made learning these topics rather difficult. So difficult in fact that you can find people who have practiced eastern practices for a lifetime and never get past the topic of the realization of the mind. My whole purpose in writing this book is to show people that the first part of eastern practices, the mind, is not as mystical as it appears to be. Once a person has the experience of the flipping of the mind then everything else falls into place.

This book does not take the place of a good teacher. Although if you were on a deserted island and only had this book you absolutely could have amazing experiences through your life using only what is in this book. A good teacher is someone who has come before you and recognizes different sign posts inside of you and can guide you away from pitfalls while giving you confirmations about your direct experience and where to go next. They help you understand your experiences by sharing their experiences and knowledge.

BASIC CONCEPTS

MEDITATION:

Meditation is a tool. And it has many psychological and physical benefits that are backed by research. There are many different ways to meditate. Some, like Zen, just have you sit there and stare off into space for the entire session. And over the course of years you will experience things similar to what Yogis experience and eventually may even slip into samadhi. Some meditations use specific breathing techniques in order to biohack their minds and bodies and drop their brainwave states to a point that makes it easier to enter into samadhi. Samadhi can be described as a type of union with the creative forces. And depending on what type of spiritual lineage a person follows there's several types of samadhi. Unfortunately samadhi is a topic all by itself that entire libraries have been written about. It is also the experience that seems to be the final realization for many practitioners. It's also possible to slip into Samadhi regularly as you've trained your brains functions to behave a certain way. Pretty much all of the big name spiritual teachers in history have experienced Samadhi. Buddha, Dogen, Yogananda and literally all of the major Indian teachers, etc. Modern spiritual teachers in western countries have often experienced forms of samadhi.

Part of meditation is helping to realize that you don't control your inner voice and thoughts. So it works throughout a practitioners life, in the beginning through to advanced realizations. When it comes to meditation I refer to a friend and mentor who is probably one of the greatest western masters in understanding meditation in both the ancient texts and in modern medical and psychological understanding. I encourage people to look him up online. His name is Forrest Knutson and he has his own Youtube channel, training, books, etc. His knowledge and wisdom about most spiritual practices, but especially karmic Yoga is amazing.

TRUE KNOWING:

The only way to know something is to have experienced it yourself. If you've ever burned your hand you know what that feels like. But try and explain what color is to a person who was born blind and no matter how good your description is they will never truly know what it's like. They can't even imagine what it's like to see because they don't have the capacity for sight to begin with. But if you understand that you don't truly know anything you've never directly experienced then you can go and look back at everything you think you know and dissect it. Where did you learn it? Was it direct experience or did someone teach it or tell it to you? Did you read it in a book? If you did then how do you know it's true? Are you accepting it as true because anything written in a book is legitimate? Says who?

If you understand this concept then you will begin to see that you actually "know" very little. But you've accepted a lot of information because it came from a source you consider to be an authority. A teacher, a parent, a religious leader, a friend, etc. But if you go deeper into it, how do they know? And you will find that it was information that they accepted from what they consider to be a trusted source. But how do we know they are trusted sources? This is where most people's minds will think that because it came from a friend, a family member, a teacher, a religious leader, etc. that those sources would never lie and would only tell you the truth. Now in reality there's a good chance that these people didn't lie to you. They simply passed on information they believe. And thus we have the longest game of "telephone" in history. Information passed down from one person to another with no direct experience of any of it. History is often written by those who win wars. And the perspective of the side that lost is almost never included. And in order to make all of the bad things our society has done to other people palatable those in positions of authority who have history written need to create an "us versus them" mentality where we are seen as the good guys and "those people" are bad guys.

So how can you trust what you are told? Don't. Question everything right down to the source and even then question the source. For me I understand that there's no way to find out the absolute truth about anything in history. All we can really do is try and go through the information objectively. But even then whatever conclusion you come to is just a belief. You can't truly "know" it.

CULTURE AND CONDITIONING:

A culture comes about after people have accepted a way of doing things. And often people don't even know why they do those things. There are many kinds of culture. Family culture, religious culture, racial culture, country culture. And even in a country there can be regional cultures. Take for example the culture in New York City versus New Orleans. Different people behaving in different ways. Because they are EXPECTED TO. And these expectations start at a young age. Your family, religious leaders, friends, society, etc. expect you to behave and believe a certain way. And failure to do so could result in mental or physical violence or being ostracized or. So we, from the time we are children, are conditioned to believe things and do things a certain way because if we don't we will be treated in a manner that makes us feel bad. This is conditioning. When an organism comes into contact with something that gives it a bad or painful experience, it begins to learn not to do that. You can also see this in relationships. If you have to tiptoe around a person for fear of how they will treat you, they have successfully conditioned you to behave in a manner that they like. Even if they don't realize what they have done because this kind of conditioning is literally instinctively learned.

So now you can begin to ask yourself why you do what you do. And 9 out of 10 times the way you are is directly attached to how other people expected you to be. If you find that you don't like to stand up or yourself or shy away from conflict, the source is often how you grew up and the way your family treated you. I'm not saying all of this is bad. It's just something for you to analyze. Morals and ethics are all forms of expected behavior society has. And they have their place. But to rise above just being a basic human who follows their programming society has given them you want to go deeper into the "why" you or society does what it does.

BELIEFS HOLD YOU BACK:

Many people will say they are "spiritual" but not actually pick up the practices found in eastern spiritual systems. They instead throw a cloak over themselves calling themselves spiritual while bashing other people who are Christian or religions. They will also attack people who don't belong to their chosen political party or ideology. They flaunt their morally superior ethics and use it as a weapon against those that they see as enemies.

All belief structures are ego. And a belief is something that is not truly known. When a true spiritual practitioner discovers themselves and their minds they come to very deep realizations. And these realizations become the basis of enlightened living. A deeply spiritual person will understand that they don't want bad things to happen to themselves. And that other people are living in this same reality experiencing much of the same things, whether or not it is pleasant or unpleasant. So they don't wish bad things on other people who don't see things their way. And they don't bash people while standing on a morally superior soapbox to justify their horrible actions.

Beliefs will hold you back from deeper truths. The more you hold onto that which you believe to be true the harder it will be for you to make the transition in your mind to true awakening. If you are willing to challenge everything you think you believe you will find that much of what you believe is simply information you accepted as true because you either trusted your source or because your mind liked the information as it reinforced it's own belief structure.

Do not come into spirituality trying to mold it to your beliefs. Instead come into it with an open mind to the possible that you know very little and are willing to discover truths even if they go against what you believe or desire. In the end you will have to be willing to give up everything to achieve your goal of understanding what you are and are not and what the reality we live in actually is.

EGO:

Ego is not what mot people think it is. Ego is often used as a description of someone who is arrogant. But ego is just what we call the inner software in our brains that's designed to keep us alive. Most people have an inner voice. This inner voice sounds like you in your own head, but it's not you. It's a problem solving software who's specific function is to take all of your experiences and memories and create scenarios in order to prevent you from getting harmed or killed. And it's almost always negative and cynical. The reason being is the evolution needed to keep you alive.

Imagine this. There's two cavemen walking through a forest. We'll call one Mr. Positive and one Mr. Negative. Mr. Positive looks up on the side of a hill and sees a cave. In front of the cave are a bunch of bones and big paw prints. Mr. Positive says "Hey man, let's go check out that cave. I bet you there's something interesting in there". Mr. Negative says "Are you crazy? If we go in there something is going to kill us and eat us. Look at the bones and the paw prints in front of the cave! If you go in there you're stupid and probably deserve whatever happens to you." Mr. Positive says "You're always so negative. There's probably nothing in there. I'm going in anyways."

If Mr. positive goes into the cave and he's wrong then he's dead. If Mr. negative is wrong and does not go into the cave anyways he's lost nothing. He still has his life. But he's gained nothing either. This inner negative feeling or inner voice is the thing inside of you that looks down a dark alley at nightnand says "Hell no, I'm not walking down there." You don't actually know if there's anything dangerous down the dark alley but your ego, the part of your brain designed to keep you alive, is creating scenarios to increase your chances of survival and it communicates this to you in the form of fear or inner voice or both.

But the problem is that this software that is designed to keep us alive doesn't have very many real problems to solve. So it creates scenarios. We don't have to hunt, fish, figure out how to grow food, survive in the winter, build shelters, create clothing from plants and animals, etc. All of these processes have been automated for us by industrialization. So we don't really have any problems. And that's a problem.........for the mind. So it creates imaginary problems that don't exist in order to try and solve them. Have you ever had an imaginary argument with someone inside your head because they said something to you that upset you? You might spend hours or even days imagining this argument. Trying to figure out how to come out on top as the victor. And then when you actually go to speak to them the conversation never goes as it did in your head. And sometimes the other person didn't even know you were upset at them.

Your mind creates imaginary scenarios that don't exist because it's trying to keep you alive and it's bored. It uses your concepts of what you think of as right and wrong in order to make judgment calls along with it's desires.

In a nutshell ego is a problem solving software designed to keep you alive by creating scenarios to predict the future. Unfortunately the person you think you are is also tied to this ego. The person you think you are is really just a collection of experiences, biases and preferences used by this automated software in order to trick you into thinking that you and it are the same. All so that it can stay in control of you. And the crazy part is that this ego KNOWS what it is and what you are and has deliberately done everything it can to keep you from figuring it out. It's like a parasitic twin living inside your head telling you dramatic stories and making you worry about the past and the future. And because you are actively listening to it your body is releasing chemicals in conjunction with it................just like when you watch TV.

When you are doing ego work you are literally trying to fight through the functions of your nervous system. My friend and mentor says that your entire nervous system is designed to keep you in a certain state of consciousness. Because that's the way our bodies are designed to work. This is why even after flipping your mind (awakening) you will still spend the rest of your life contending with your mind. Even Buddha recognized this. He just decided he would never be deceived by it again.

DUHKHA:

Duhkha is a Sanskrit word that translates to suffering, pain or unhappiness. A better understanding of it for our modern minds would be "never satisfied. Always seeking". Duhkha is a condition of how the mind behaves with desires for what it wants and doesn't want. "If I only had the right job, the right amount of money, the right car, the right house, the right spouse, if people would live the way I think is right.............then I could be happy" It also works for what you don't want. "I don't want to be treated badly. I don't want you to do this because I think it's wrong. Etc."

The always seeking, never satisfied nature of the mind can be seen in life. If you've ever really wanted to buy something expensive and you finally saved up enough to buy it, what happens after you buy it? When you first get it you get that happy, ecstatic feeling. Almost like a drug. You get a boost of dopamine. Then after a while that "new" feeling wears off. Often in a matter of days. Then you're looking to buy something else. There's that yearning of wanting something else. Often people don't realize they are self medicating this way. They may go shopping and call it retail therapy. They might self medicate with sex. Bounce from relationship to relationship always looking for the person they imagine will make them happy. If a person has duhkha really bad you'll see them bounce from relationship to relationship, job to job, pick up and move to a new area. They will say things like "I just need a fresh start." But no matter where you go, there you are. It's usually not the situation that needs to change but the person's perspectives on life itself.

Duhkha is the reason why we have wars and conflicts with other people, countries, religions, etc. It is THE driving force for personal suffering. And personal suffering affects other people around you. If you have people in power with severe duhka then you get a leader that says "If I had your resources, your land, if your people practiced my religion, if they paid money to me………..then the world would be a better place. Power hungry people are mired in duhkha. In this format EGO uses the "greater good" in order to justify how it treats other people. And you can see this in our world today. People standing up on pulpits saying "I need you to vote for me because I will do "this" for the "greater good" and THOSE PEOPLE OVER THERE don't want you to have what you want. So they are the enemy!"

Duhkha uses your desires for things like justice, right and wrong, world peace, etc. in order to justify how it gets you to treat other people. Duhkha is how people justify fraud and theft. They want something, so they do it and come up with excuses why it's not that bad. Same thing with how people treat other people. "Those people don't have my values, and I'm a great person. So they must be evil or bad..........therefore I'm justified in treating them a certain way."

Evil is not some easy to spot thing with a big sign on it that says EVIL. Evil is what people do to each other every day. And evil starts in the mind. It is the mind that convinces you it's okay to treat other people you don't like badly and justifies the means. Evil is what you do. To wish harm on someone, to directly or indirectly and knowingly do something to harm someone else. It could be financial, reputation, physical, etc. But it all starts in the mind. I want. I don't want. If other people would just do what I know to be the right way then the world would be a better place. Some people have created spiritual boogie men to give themselves a way out of holding themselves and their thoughts accountable. And you will see this all the time. Shifting blame of why they do what they do onto something else. Why take accountability for your thoughts and actions when you can blame the devil?

THE MIND / BODY CONNECTION:

What you think about affects how you feel. If you are watching a scary movie, you know it's not real. YOU KNOW IT"S NOT REAL. Yet your body still releases stress hormones like adrenaline and cortiisol. Something in the movie jumps out at you and you jump as if it's happening to you in real life. Why does this happen? It's the mind body connection. Whatever you think about your body adjusts to. It's a part of the fight or flight system, relaxation system etc. On the reverse. If you watch a funny movie or video your body releases feel good chemicals and you relax and your blood pressure goes down.

What you think about causes your body to release chemicals as if it's happening right now. The body itself doesn't have it's own logic system in the traditional sense. So it relies on what the brain tells it is going on in order to respond accordingly. So if your mind is constantly making you think about something bad that happened in the past you may experience this as depression. If the mind worries about the future you may experience anxiety. But here's the problem. You can't control the future. And because it can't be predicted 100% of the time the mind keeps up this loop of anxiety. It's trying to solve a problem that can't be solved. And the ego can't stand problems that can't be solved. That's what's happening to people that are addicted to conspiracy theories. Since there's no way to truly verify if the conspiracy is true or not the mind just keeps running around in circles working itself up into a tizzy. And then they get mad when other people don't share in their fear. In all honesty there's probably not much the average person can do to stop two major countries from going into nuclear war with each other. So why spend your entire life worrying about a doomsday scenario that you have no control over.

Another interesting condition of the mind is what is referred to as placebo effect. But unfortunately it is looked at in a negative light. As if the people who experience it are somehow not intelligent. Placebo effect is amazing. To believe that you are taking a certain medication and get the positive effects from it without any of the negative side effects. If science could tap into this as a potential treatment supplement then who knows how far it could go. People like Joe Dispenza are putting in time and effort in order to help train people to tap into and use their mind body connection to help themselves. Not to mention that people with positive attitudes do better at healing in hospitals.

WHAT TRAUMA ACTUALLY IS:

Trauma is an event in your life that created a deep seated fear. This fear caused your ego (if you don't know the real meaning of ego then please read the other articles about that) to become afraid of the same thing happening again. And since ego is an automated problem solver it keeps trying to figure out how to prevent similar future events. In order to try and solve this problem it thinks about the event..... a lot. But because we don't actually have control of anything and because of the potential for chaos to ruin any well made plans, your subconscious can't figure out a way to 100% stop the same event from happening again. So it continues to chew on the problem, always trying to figure out how to prevent it from happening. So it's a vicious cycle of thinking, which creates more fear, anxiety, depression, etc. Your mind also begins to associate certain things with the memory of the event. These are triggers. A certain thing happens or gets said and your mind thinks about the painful event again.

Here's what thoughts do to the body. If you watch a scary movie your body releases adrenaline and other stress hormones. If you watch a comedy your body releases feel good hormones and your stress hormones go down. And you know that what you are seeing on TV is not real. It's not actually happening. Yet you still get chemical releases from it. The exact same thing happens to you when you relive memories in your head. Your body doesn't know the difference between what is real and what your mind is thinking about. And chronic stress hormones floating through your body all the time causes health problems. Both physical and mental.

So what can you do to change this and get out of the slavery of mental suffering? First you have to be able to clearly understand ego and what it does to you. Then you have to pick up a practice to separate yourself from your ego and live your life free from its controlling influence.

If I tell people that living with trauma is a choice, that they are willingly holding onto it and could change it by changing their mental habits they will often get angry, say that you don't know what real trauma is or what is like to live with it, etc. But unfortunately, what is written here is true. It is scientifically proven. And there are various methods to get freedom from trauma. But like the old saying says : If you believe you can't, you're right. If you believe you can, you're right.

So if people are given the knowledge and the tools to get out of their own suffering, why don't people actually do it? Maybe they have to suffer enough before they are ready to look for the answers.

THE FLIPPING OF THE MIND.

In Zen there is a concept called the gateless gate. It's where your perspective flips and you can see the mind clearly and what it does to you. Plato recognized this flip in perspective and created a story called the Allegory of the Cave in order to try and shed some light onto it. I'll give you a basic story of the Allegory of the Cave and then I will give my own story to supplement it. The real story of the Allegory of the Cave is long but it is brilliant.

Imagine that you are a slave. You are chained side by side with other slaves facing a wall inside of a cave. You have lived in this cave your entire life. The only thing thing you know about the world is by the shadows cast on the wall in front of you. Then one day your chains break and you go outside and see the world exactly the way it is and you are in awe. Everything you thought you knew about the world was so very different. You rush back inside and try to tell the other slaves about what the real world looks looks like but they attack you verbally and physically. They do not want to leave the world that they know.

The allegory of the cave shows us a contrast between what we thought we knew versus what we see once our mind flips over. The original story goes even further into the social problems that arise to a person once this perspective change happens. How that person can be seen as crazy or stupid. And to truly awakened beings, they can be seen as crazy or socially awkward. And often these people, many who walk among you in everyday life, keep quiet about their experience because society does punish those that do not conform to societal norms of thinking or religious beliefs.

Now, the story I came up with is more of a direct interpretation of my experience with this mental phenomenon. People I know that have experienced this usually agree with it.

Imagine that you are in a prison cell. You don't know how long you've been in the cell but it's been years. There is a guard that stands around the cell door and taunts you. This guard seems to know everything about you. He knows all of your secrets, your insecurities, your fears. And he uses this information to mentally torture you. One day while the guard is standing in front of your cell door telling you all sorts of awful things and threats of bad things to come to you you begin to pace back and force frantically. You've gone to the point of mentally breaking. You don't know how much more you can take it. While pacing frantically you trip over yourself and stumble into the cell door. The cell door swings open and even *through* guard standing in front of the door. You realize that the guard is just a projection on the wall. The sound of his voice is speakers located somewhere. But the guard isn't actually there. You cautiously wander through the prison and find nobody else there. No doors are locked either. You walk out of the front doors of the prison and turn around and look back at it. Nobody rushes out to capture you. Nobody shoots at you. You then realize that the only thing keeping you in that prison............was you. Because you thought there was no way out. And you laugh for a good long time. Then you cry. And then you look out into the world and you see there are other prisons around you with people inside of them just like you were.

This mental phenomenon is very real. And it often comes from a mental break of some kind. As we go through life suffering we take on all of this mental and emotional pressure. And then one day a crack forms. We don't know what's going on but something is happening to us. And when we have reached a certain point where we don't know how much more we can take and we're willing to do anything to achieve peace, something begins to point us in certain directions.

Sometimes this mental break can happen from extreme trauma, near death experiences, actual mental breaks, high doses of psychedelics, etc. There is a small percentage of people that this just happens to spontaneously without a break. They just one day wake up to their own mind. They find that the person they think they are doesn't exist. And it scares them.

THE FALLING AWAY OF YOU:

Once you get to a certain point of seeing your mind there is a condition that often happens where you begin to see that everything you do in life is to either satisfy the standards that other people have laid down in societal expectations, or to satisfy your own ego. When this began to happen to me I stopped going to the gym. I realized that the only reason I was lifting weights was to impress women and have guys envy or fear me. And I lost all motivation to go. I stopped lifting for almost a year and a half. I now go to the gym because I need to keep my body healthy. So I have very different motivations now.

SO NOW WHAT?

These are some pretty heavy topics. And it can cause a lot of mixed feelings. This is normal. Something inside of us knows much of this already. We may have even stopped at times and asked ourselves why we did a certain thing. We may have even watched our inner voice take over and do something as if we were just a passenger in our own body. So, what do you do now? Well, it's time to get into the science of rewiring our brains and get us to see our own minds clearly. This is a very important step in a true spiritual aspirant. We can pick up habits that ease our suffering and eventually swing us in the other direction in order to become happy. And as our mind flips over and we enter the gateless gate then the real journey begins.

REWIRING THE BRAIN TO BE HAPPY:

Your mind is an amazing tool. Whatever you practice over and over again you get better at until you've mastered it. Most people have mastered being negative, sad, depressed, etc. So what we have to do is begin mental patterns that overwrite our current patterns. And to do that we need to understand theta brain waves and how conditioning works.

When you first wake up in the morning and you're still half asleep you're in theta brain wave mode. This is an excellent time to get information directly into your subconscious. It's like when you're running late and you jumped right out of bed and drive to work while listening to the radio. Whatever song was on the radio while you were still half asleep now runs through your mind all day. We're going to use this to our advantage by using mantra programming. Notice how I said programming? Because that's what mantras are. They get information and directions into your subconscious in order to elicit a change or response. But to make it more powerful we need to say our mantra out loud. This way the sound of the words comes back to your ears and feeds it back into your mind making it more powerful than just thoughts. And we need to be specific and careful with the choice of the words we want to use to program our mind. For example, never say "I am NOT insecure". Your mind heard "I" and "insecure". Instead say "I am confident". This program will give you the results you want without internal conflict. So if we are trying to rewire our brain to be positive we can use a word program like "Today is a good day. It's a beautiful day. It's a positive day. Today I am centered and will stay centered. I am positive and will stay positive. And I have a shield around me that protects me from negative and bad." This sets the intention of your mind for the day and harnesses the subconscious power of expectation. You want to say your morning mantra at least ten times out loud. This will make it's way into your subconscious and begin reprogramming it.

Next we want to set your chemical mood for the day using conditioning. Think of the power of conditioning using Pavlov's dogs. What you do begins to have an automatic effect on your body. What I did was I would watch funny squirrel videos on my phone. Or babies laughing. This caused me to laugh and get a release of good chemicals. It also became a part of my routine so as soon as I woke up my mind began to expect to laugh and feel good and started becoming automatic and my new reality. This also set the mood for the day and the rest of my day seemed to go a lot smoother.

Now the final part of rewiring yourself to be positive is to watch your thoughts. If you catch yourself having negative thoughts then you force yourself to think of three positive thoughts and overwrite the negative. I would have three thoughts already ready to go just for this. Such as something funny that my son said or did. And throughout the day I would just make this automatic. Have a negative thought? Think of three positive thoughts. It's hard at first but it does get easier. But if you want to tap into some real magic here then you want to think about a thought that begins to release good emotion inside of you. Don't just think of a random thought. Try and feel the thought. Like if you were to think about your child doing something funny or amazing that brings that good feeling up. You want to *feel* your positive idea or emotion. You can use outside assistance by playing a song that make you feel good.

Or watching a video. This practice of shifting your thoughts to feel good is extremely important in the long run. We can eventually tap into this at will. Imagine being able to enter into a state where you feel love out of nowhere for no reason. Tapping into this is powerful and can even affect the energy in a room.

What happens when you begin this regimen is that within a week you will begin to see and feel a difference. And this will excite you and make you want to keep going. So keep going. Within a month you won't recognize yourself anymore as the programming and conditioning takes over. In three months you have a solid base for happiness. Of course there's much more to dealing with life than this. But this is where you start.

Here is a quick reference guide for this daily practice.

OK. So begin to see your mind and changing yourself from a negative mentality to a positive mentality is the key to becoming happy. But it means you have to adopt a daily practice. I've written about the science of how these techniques work in the article Rewiring the Brain. You can find it using the search option on this page or look for the announcements section.

Nothing about what I show people is new. It's very old methods going back thousands of years. The only thing I did was reframe it for the modern mind and use what we have in our modern world. These techniques are backed by science using brain wave states and conditioning. There's nothing mystical about it. To simplify the process I will list the 3 steps below. If you can make it a daily habit for 30 days you will find yourself experiencing good days and changes within the first week or two. This will excite your and you'll become glad to do the practice. If you want to read about how the techniques work in depth, check out the Rewiring the Brain article I wrote.

1. When you first wake up. You must say it out loud for it to have a deeper affect on your subconscious while you're in theta brainwave state. Say this ten times.

"Today is a good day. It's a beautiful day. It's a positive day. Today I am positive and will stay positive. I am centered and will stay centered. And I have a shield around me that protects me from negative and bad."

2. Next, spend 10-15 minutes watching funny videos on YouTube. You want to find something that makes you laugh. This releases good chemicals in the brain and gets your day started on a highly positive note.

3. When you have a negative thought, replace those thoughts with three positive thoughts. It's easier if you

already have three thoughts ready to go. Something that makes you smile, or laugh or feel good. This begins to change the inner voice to be less negative. But you really need to focus on this part. Don't just think of something random or some words. You want to *feel* the thoughts. I like to think about my dog, or my son. These bring good feelings and I can feel the chemical release happening inside me. This is where the true magic is. *Feel* it.

If you want you can make a mark on a calendar to give you a visual gauge of the progress you make. You can also write down your experiences in a journal. But only write your experiences and how you handled them. And don't focus on "I want / I don't want" or negative things. If you have a negative thought just write down the basis of what it was then how you handled it and brought yourself back to being centered or happy. Do not constantly write about anything negative. This will reinforce negativity in your mind. Focus on the positive.

If you want to pick up a meditation practice you can. It will only benefit you. But dedicate some time to this practice. Watch your mind as it creates doubts and fears out of nowhere. I'm going to list some information about the mind and it's behaviors. Besides the daily practice it's good to periodically read about these ego layers and conditions of the mind. The more you ponder the mind and observe what it does, the better the conditions you create for the flipping of the mind.

These 3 daily exercises seem simple enough. And that's the problem. People's minds expect something complicated and expensive in order to work. But there is the devil in the details. It's the mind telling you it's too simple or it won't work. I have helped a lot of people put an end to depression, anxiety, PTSD, trauma and live happy lives. This simple 3 step daily routine may be simple. But it's powerful. In India there are people who only say one mantra their entire lives. And everything they need comes from that. So simple is good. And this method is just an updated method that our modern western scientifically trained minds will understand.

EXPERIENCE, COINCIDENCE, BELIEF AND KNOWING:

Experience, coincidence, belief, knowing. The power of true knowing and how to get there.

Many people believe many things. But how much of what they believe is actually true? And how do you apply it to your spiritual practice? If you have directly experienced something then you actually know about it. For example, if you have ever burned your hand then you know what it feels like. But if you try and describe color to someone who was blind from birth then your descriptions, no matter how well you think you articulate it, can never truly be known by the blind person. The same thing happens in a spiritual practice. Often we are told something or read something in a book. If it's mystical in nature our modern mind will suspect it of being BS. Which is good and normal. So what ends up happening is an evolution of not knowing to knowing. And I mean true knowing.

For example. You tell someone that if they want to be happy they can rewire their brain by applying some techniques. Say for example, before they get out of bed they repeat a mantra ten times of "Today is a good day, it's a positive day, it's a beautiful day. Today I am positive and happy." Then you tell them that they should spend the first 10 or 15 minutes after that watching funny videos on youtube about squirrels. The negative mind is going to say "This is some hooky BS". But................if they actually start doing it, consistently, they begin to create different thinking patterns. These thinking patterns begin to rewire the brain. They notice (experience) that their day was better than normal. They think it's a coincidence. But if they keep going they notice that more often than not their days have been positive. And so coincidence turns into actual patterns. Then they begin to believe. But belief is still not the end game. As they continue the practice those patterns that have formed become their new normal. And then one day they wake up and they "know". Truly know. And their life is forever changed.

It's like this with everything in life. We experience something, begin to see a consistent pattern with it, begin to believe it and then know it. And the best part is that this pattern of learning can be used in all aspects of anything spiritual, or mystical, or just plain old psychological. Want to test the power of mantras? Do the mantra for a month and see what happens. If something doesn't work for you, then move on to something else. Each person perceives things differently. Like how some people like the taste of black licorice and some people hate it. (Black licorice is the devil's flavor in my opinion. Absolutely disgusting).

So, in monasteries around the world that's why a specific exercise is practiced for months or years at a time, or even a lifetime. So, what are you trying to achieve? And how can you use the understanding of this tool to achieve your goal?

Note: There is a big difference between real "knowing" and false knowing. There are people who know quite a bit about stuff that just isn't true. Remember to keep the idea of real knowing (direct experience) separate from knowledge gained from reading, videos, social media posts, etc. I

PONDERING THE ORIGINS OF YOUR THOUGHTS

When you are doing the daily work that I prescribe people the third technique is to watch your mind and change your thoughts from negative to something positive. And this causes your brain to release the good feeling chemicals that shift how you feel. But there's something deeper here. To catch your thoughts. When you're just going about your day and your mind just throws a random negative thought into the mix, did you catch it? Or did you see the thought and fall into it and start thinking about it. The mind is compulsive. A part of realizing your own mind is catching these thoughts when they happen and ask yourself "Did I actually want to think about that thought? Or did it just pop in here out of nowhere". If you spend time during the day doing this then eventually you are going to have the mental flip I speak about. This right here is actually harder than just saying morning mantras and watching videos. Watching your own mind is the hard part. But the more you do it, the more you catch it, the more you get closer to this really big realization.

You do not completely control your thoughts. It does things on it's own.

And you can't get your mind to completely stop. You need your mind to function. Your ego is also the interface to this world. If you were completely devoid of ego then you would have pure awareness looking out of your body but you wouldn't know what food was, how to eat, how to speak, etc. You would be in a form of aware vegetative state. And this can be achieved by some people doing certain types of meditation. But it's not a good state to be in.

A WARNING:

I have helped people achieve awakening only to watch them fall back into their own minds. There's many reasons for this but I'm going to list a couple of them that seem to be common.

There's a trick of the ego that is absolutely terrible. After an awakening a person thinks "Now that I'm aware of my mind it can't trick me again. So I want to go do............."

And the bad part is that you can't convince them it's pulled them back in. A sign that it's got them is that they go back to doing all their old habits. They are back into drama and romantic ideas. They may post all sorts of stuff on social media about "spiritual" stuff, lessons they want other people to learn, their likes and dislikes, what they think the world needs to do, etc. And they refuse to do more internal work. They just think they've got a handle on everything and that's it.

The second common problem is that a person just wanted to achieve the end of suffering. Now that they aren't having their mind make their lives hell they go back to "I want". They get sucked into desires. This is where you see people who are codependent think they aren't codependent yet they will start seeking another person to be in their lives soon after. Or they will chase money. Or fall into chasing mysticism. The mind loves mysticism. It seeks to control life for it's own desires.

Mysticism brings the promise of wealth, abundance, happiness, health, predicting the future, etc. But mysticism is just tools. If a person is very well centered in themselves and have a good control of their ego and a high level of understanding of their existence and how it affects others, then mysticism is just a tool they might use to help someone or themselves. Healing is a good thing. But ego and it's desires now seeks to make lots of money using it's new found powers and then it lies to itself and says "I'm helping people". No. If someone is broke down on the side of the road with a flat tire and you help them change that tire, you are helping them. But if you are a tow truck service that charges fees to do the job then you are providing a service. Never let your mind get the two mixed up. It's okay to have a service to provide something people want. It's a job. And we all need money to eat and pay our bills. But never get it confused with helping people. Think of all of the times people have truly helped you and didn't want anything in return. Then think of people who offered to "help" you for a cost.

I watched a person I helped go back into their belief structures. They didn't truly *know* the things they believed. But they didn't want to challenge their own beliefs or even give up the beliefs until they found out for themselves. They just fell back into their old life and old habits. The only difference is that they believed they were free of their minds. Many people, especially in the western countries, are all about instant gratification. They don't want to do the hard work. So, getting over their basic level of suffering is the end of the line for them. They just want their old lives back, minus the suffering.

PART 2

LIVING AN AWAKENED LIFE

Welcome to the second part of this book. I'm going to be honest when I say that while some of this may make sense to you prior to the flipping of your mind, the majority of it might not. There's a reason why so many ancient phrases and sayings sound like Chinese fortune cookies to our western minds. Most of the ancient teachings are esoteric. Esoteric teachings mean that there has to be a certain level of comprehension in a certain subject to be understood. There are even esoteric teachings in the Bible, despite the damage the Roman's did to it during their takeover of the religion in 325AD and years after. In this case the only way to truly understand the depth of eastern spirituality is through flipping the mind. Once this happens then many other things start to make sense.

There is no order for what is written in this second part of the book. That's because there is no straight line in anyone's spiritual path. What is needed will find you. And so you will get exactly what you need when you need it.

If you've ever heard the phrase "The world is a reflection of who you are inside." this is an esoteric teaching. What it means is that as you become peaceful, as the layers of the mind fall away, as you become happy, and as your perspective shifts you begin to notice that life seems to get easier. Bad things seem to disappear, more good things start to happen for you, opportunities arise that get you out of bad environments and into healthy environments. Your relationships change. People that are toxic or manipulative start to leave you alone and good people come into your life.

To the logical mind one would think that this is just a simple case of seeing how people really are and creating healthy boundaries. But to the awakened mind you realize you're not doing anything at all. It's all happening on it's own. This is where you begin to really "see" that life is not what it appears to be at first glance. That the reality we live in is not some rigid structure made out of atoms and science. You see that there's some sort of symbiotic relationship between yourself (consciousness) and this very interactive system we dwell in. There's an intelligence deep within everything. Hidden in plain site. And so you truly begin your journey on the spiritual path. The life lessons and wisdom you gain here will continue until your body passes away and your consciousness goes to the next level of existence.

So, if you have not flipped your mind over yet, that's okay. You can read and enjoy what is here. But once your mind does flip, come back to this part of the book and you will find you see it very differently.

YOU ARE ALLOWED TO CHANGE:

As a person progresses many changes will happen. And some people in your life may not like it. They may make comments such as "I don't like this new you that you're becoming." And the reason is simple. They are losing control of you and they aren't getting what they want out of you. Everyone is allowed to change for the better, including you. You do not need anyone's permission. This could also mean that you will lose people in your life and you may need to create boundaries.

If a person tells you something to the effect of "I know who you really are. People can't truly change. You will always be............" then what they are doing is trying to manipulate you in order to keep you down or in their control. Think about this. If a person does something in their past and then changes, whatever is in their past is gone. They are allowed to change to become a better person. If anyone tries to box you into your past actions or thinks you can't ever be forgiven then that means they can't be either. That means everything they have ever done wrong is who they are right now. But if you tell this to them and they think this doesn't apply to them, then you've found a highly manipulative person and a hypocrite.

You do not have to conform to the boxes of other people's minds.

FORGIVENESS AND BLESSING IS MAGIC:

In our lives there have been people who have done bad things to us. I know from my life and others I know that people are capable of absolutely horrible things. And the idea of forgiving someone who has done something heinous to you doesn't seem possible and you probably don't want to forgive them. But here's what happens inside of you.

Forgiveness isn't about giving a person a free pass for the bad things they've done. It's about cutting yourself free from the memories inside of you. Holding onto a bad memory and a grudge of the person who has hurt you creates an actual physical bond in your mind that causes triggers. Just like when I was talking about trauma and ego. To let of that grudge and forgive a person for their past crimes cuts you loose from them in a physical, mental and spiritual way.

If you allow the memory of what someone has done to you to linger inside of you then you are allowing them to victimize you effortlessly. But what about them? Don't they have to apologize? Seeking closure is something the mind desires immensely. So let's do a thought experiment. Let's pretend that you have a family member who did something heinous to you. The kind of bad stuff that gets people put in prison. Let's pretend that you decide to go to them and maybe even the family and demand that they admit to what they've done and apologize. And what if they do apologize? Will your mind accept it or demand more? What if they don't admit to it? Will your family back you up or start a high level of drama in order to protect that person and the family's image?

What was done to you is terrible. And I'm not encouraging anyone to stay quiet if something like this has happened to them. And we do have a criminal justice system (although very broken) that may be able to render justice for what they have done. But now what? Keep holding onto the memory and the hate and allow it to poison you? The best revenge anyone could ever have is to be so free of the past and the influence of other people that you can rarely ever think about them and when you do it's a fleeting thought that doesn't bother you.

On the philosophical side of spiritual practice there is a deeper realization that can occur. A person who is not truly awakened does not comprehend what they have done in the same way you do. They may not even care. They are asleep, living in the land of ego. For if they knew what they were or what they had truly done then they themselves would be changed. Unfortunately we do not get to decide to wake other people up. Life decides when and where. And you can see this when a person who has done bad things has a near death experience. They may come back from it, pick up religion, make apologies and attempt to change for the better.

If you have had very bad things happen to you just know that there are other people out here in this world who have a depth of understanding and compassion and can help you. You are not alone. And once you are given the keys to life through awakening and the spiritual path you will transform into an amazing form of energy that will touch the lives of other people. I do not look back at my past life and feel sorry for myself or wish that it never happened. I realize that the pain and suffering I went through was the flame that forged me into what I am today. And I will say something that may not even make sense to you. The bad things I went through were absolutely necessary. I could not have become what I am without it. And if you understand this concept then you may grasp the idea of Yin and Yang. Light and Dark. But it's all a part of the same whole.

EGO. AN IN DEPTH ANALYSIS OF WHAT YOU ARE NOT:

Ego. That terrible word people hate. Yet most people don't know what the word really means. Or what it is and how it affects your life. Ego is much more complex than just the basic description of it. In simple terms your ego is your persona. It is an accumulation of your experiences that make you..... you. But that's not really you.

You see, the ego is more than just your experiences. It is an automated problem solving software designed to keep you alive. It is an evolutionary trait that allows you to predict problems and come up with a solution for it. It uses abstract thinking to connect the dots. It is your inner voice you hear talking. But guess what. IT IS NOT YOU. That's right. That voice you hear inside your head? It's not you. Never was. You just thought it was. And your "ego" let you think that so it could stay in control of you. You don't believe that your inner voice is not you? Try sitting for 5 minutes and not having any thoughts. See how long it takes you to start day dreaming, thinking of different scenarios, having inner voice dialog, etc. Most people can't last 30 seconds without a thought.

And guess what else? Your ego, your inner voice, is not your friend. Think about it like an evil Siri or Alexa inside your head. Or the evil step sisters in Cinderella. Let's analyze how it acts.

* Most people's inner voice is almost always negative. It says things like "I'm not good enough. I'm not attractive enough. I'm not where I want to be in life. If I only had 'this' I would be happy."
* A lot of people have imaginary arguments inside their heads with someone that upset them. Do you know how crazy that sounds? If you talk to someone outside of your head who is not there we call that schizophrenia. If we have imaginary fights and arguments with people in our heads we call that normal.
* What your mind thinks about your body responds to. This is the mind / body connection. It's so strong that what you see on TV causes your body to release chemicals that affect your body. If you watch a scary movie your body releases stress hormones and your blood pressure rises. Something jumps out on screen and you jump too and have an adrenaline dump. Even when you KNOW it's not real.
* Your ego knows everything about you. Your secrets. Your insecurities. Your past trauma. Everything you have ever experienced.
* Your ego has no shame. It will manipulate you using your fears, insecurities, traumas and more against you. It does this to stay in control of you. People who are easily upset are easily controlled.

* Your ego will cause you to second guess yourself. And it definitely causes overthinking.
* Your ego is never satisfied. It's always seeking something outside of itself that it believes will make it happy. This condition of the ego is called Dukkha. It's what causes people to bounce from relationship to relationship, job to job and move from place to place. One of the most common phrases of Dukkha in our time is "I just need a fresh start".
* Your ego is not your friend.

So what do you do with this information? Well first you have to pay attention to your thoughts, discover what is something you've directly experienced versus what you thought. Catch yourself in the moment when your thoughts run away.
On a side note I am going to give my experience on another topic that directly ties into ego and why I don't like to use certain words. Ego work is the same as "shadow work". Same thing. But to me there's a built in mind trap in the word Shadow Work. I see people all the time talk about doing shadow work. Here's the problem with it. The words "shadow work" are appealing to the mind (ego) because it sounds cooler than ego. Plus to acknowledge your own ego makes your ego uncomfortable. It shines a direct light on the source of all suffering. Secondly, "shadow work" is the new boogie man. It allows you to put blame on the idea of a force that is somehow out of your own control. It relieves the person of responsibility of their own actions and thoughts. You want to know what the devil is? It's

your ego. Everything evil that comes from people is because of ego. That's why they created the devil. To shift blame to something outside of themselves because it's easier to blame outside forces than to take responsibility for your own evil thoughts.

Show me a person that promotes "Shadow work" and you'll see someone who never got past their own issues and moved on to the next phase of spiritual evolution. They didn't realize just how sneaky their own mind was and how it uses concepts to keep you trapped. Someone out there is going to be upset that I said this and they'll want to argue against it. And that's when the ego will expose itself. It feels hurt. Upset. It doesn't like what I have to say. And then it will attack.

PAVLOV'S DOGS AND EMOTIONS:

In the first stages of ending our suffering we have to take a proactive approach to rewiring our brains and our body response. But because many people have spent years in negative cycles and thoughts they have "mastered" the art of negativity and the body's physical response to those thoughts and emotional states have become reflexive and almost instantaneous. To understand why it's important to have a daily practice we will take a look at Pavlov's dogs.

Pavlov was a scientist who was studying conditioned behavior. He had a theory that dogs could associate being fed with the sound of a bell and could be trained to salivate just by hearing the sound of the bell, even without any food present. And his theory was proven right. After conditioning the dogs they would begin to salivate just by hearing the bell. Your body does the same thing.

If you spend much of your time worrying, having negative thoughts, stressing, etc. then your body 's natural response will be to release stress hormones. And most people have gotten really good at it. So a part of the necessary personal training to become happy and not suffer requires you to condition your body response to your thoughts...... but in a positive way.

When I was first learning this I used to wake up and lay in the bed saying positive mantras out loud such as "today is a good day. It's a positive day. I'm going to be happy and negativity won't stick to me" followed by watching funny videos on YouTube for ten or fifteen minutes. Within days the conditioning began to work and the "feel good" hormones began to come on faster. Even more if I imagine laying in bed, laughing at funny videos of squirrels being their crazy selves I can feel the happiness and joy start to pick up. I conditioned myself to associate good thoughts with a good hormone release. Bruce Lipton and Joe Dispenza are two well known modern teachers who specifically teach this. And if you've never seen the documentary called E-motion then you should check it out.

It's very important to take the time and effort to tap into and use your natural happy hormones. Because stress and depression lead to reduced immune response and can cause actual damage to the cells in your brain.

Not doing anything is still making a choice. If a person doesn't put in any serious effort into this then they are still choosing to feel bad. There are some people in life with legitimate mental health issues that cause problems with the brain and feeling emotion. But every person I've ever directly spoken with I've been able to get them to feel joy and happiness using their thoughts.

You have the power to be happy.

VOICE MAGIC AND VIBRATIONAL ENERGY:

We have all heard about mantras, chanting, japa and spells. Fewer have heard about hesychasm. There is a reason that buddhists, mystic Christians, Sufis, Sihks, Native Americans, shamans, etc use songs and chanting. Vibrational energy with intent. To understand this I have to go into a little bit of science.

Everything you think is solid.........is not. If you look at atoms there is a vast amount of space from one atom to the next. It's so vast that if an atom was the size of a period on a piece of paper there would be over a mile of space inbetween to the next atom. In other words, you have more space inside of you than actual matter. And matter itself is not even really solid. It's energy that has been brought down to a lower frequency using a master frequency. This master frequency is also a phenomenon that confounds scientists. This master vibration is constant. It doesn't get lower or higher. It doesn't take a break or go away. The ancients called it the word of God. The greeks called it Logos. And it sounds like....Om.

So science has already caught light waves in the middle of transforming into matter. They have even taken photos of it in action. So, literally, everything you see is nothing more than light at various stages of vibration. This is not some wishful thinking. It is something that modern science is catching up on.

Now for those who have been in a spiritual practice long enough you may have discovered what you are, or aren't. And you may have felt the presence of an intelligent........something. And you may have come to the conclusion that everything, and I mean everything, is literally all a part of one larger creation. So how can voice create an affect on this.......reality?

Your consciousness is extremely powerful. We view it as limited by our physical body. But the consciousness itself is unlimited. We may not be able to see it due to Maya (the illusion that we see) but it is very powerful. In order to create an affect on this "divine matrix" of energy we have to have intent. So, when we think of something as if it has happened and then apply emotion to it we get what is called manifesting. Well, mantras, chanting and singing are also a way to broadcast energy and intent into the divine matrix to affect change.

Voice energy is powerful for beginners because it's easier to believe something is happening when you feel it physically thanwhen you just think about something. So when you start a spiritual practice that tells you to perform mantras or affirmations that's what is going on. Whether or not you believe it you are still pushing intent out into the divine matrix using sound waves. And energy is the universal language. The words we use are tied to meanings and therefore carry code of what we are trying to do. Some believe that Sanscrit is a language that is more powerful than others because the words were derived from universally obtained sources. I don't know if this is true. But I know that anyone can use any language, including thoughts to affect change.

There was a Japanese scientist named Masaru Emoto who studied the affects of spoken words into water. He would then freeze the water and look at the ice crystals. What he found was the positive speech created pristine, beautiful crystals. While negative speach created mishapen or ugly or unclear crystals. Think about that next time you start saying negative words to someone. It has an affect on a molecular level.

So if you want to affect change on yourself, even if you don't believe in mantras, give it a try. People that I have told this to usually see changes within a week. More within a month. Until they either rewire their brain or achieve what they are trying to do.

TRUTH VERSUS NON TRUTH:

Want to know a secret? Something you probably didn't know existed that you have access to? Want to understand how to tell the difference between what is true and what is not? Then you're looking for the power of discernment. To understand discernment you have to understand a couple things.

Truth versus non truth. Notice I didn't say lies, I said non truth. A person can tell you something they truly believe but it's not true. And they aren't lying. Even you have believed things at one time that weren't true and told other people about it.
Truth has no feeling. The way people think is literally backwards from what reality is. When we scan for the truth we are looking for a sign that tells us it's the truth. But in reality the truth has no signs. No sensations. The truth is already perfect. It doesn't need anything.

Non truth on the other hand does have ways of letting know its there. That's why your gut let's you know when someone is lying to you or telling you something that feels "off". I show people a way to calibrate themselves to both truth and non truth.
Look at your hand. While looking at your hand pay attention to your mind. If I say "that is your hand" feel what your mind is doing. Your mind should be blank,

calm, no sensations. But if I say that politicians don't lie....... feel how your mind reacts to it. There's something in the back of your mind that flares up. It's noticeable. That is one way to figure out how to calibrate yourself to discern truth from non truth.

THE GHOST OF YOU VERSUS WHO YOU ARE NOW:

As you progress down your path you will come across a very unexpected obstacle that can cause serious discomfort. It's where people that know you see you change, but then try and keep you locked into the person you were. They might tease you or make fun of you for being happier and more positive. They might directly attack your spiritual practice and that you'll never achieve your goals. Some will claim that you're a fraud because they remembered the way you used to behave in the past.

Unfortunately not everyone in our life is meant to be with us through our entire life. It could be friends, family, co-workers, etc. If you keep changing you will lose people. They will be bitter. You will be attacked. It is your choice of how much exposure to negative and toxic people you choose to accept. Eventually you will realize that you will have outgrown some of those people. They will find their way out of your life one way or another.

Do not allow your past to keep you in the prison of who you were. The people who would use your past against you are like the prison guards of your own mind.

CONFIDENCE IS EGO:

Only the ego tells you you're not good enough. Only it cares what other people think. Remove that and what you are left with is what you mistake as confidence. It's not. Real confidence is just not being worried about what people think. And that gives you the ability to do what you need to to do without fear of judgment.

FIND THE SOURCE OF YOUR AWARENESS:

If you are aware of things like your inner voice, think about that. You are aware of your inner voice. So try and turn your awareness to itself. You are aware of your body, the environment and your own mind. So.........what is this awareness that is aware? And why can you not find it but it's obviously there? Dig deep on this. Spend lots of time on this.

TRUE VIRTUES VERSUS THE CLOAK OF EGO:

Many people pick up the virtue of empathy and compassion. To someone who doesn't understand the depth behind this they picked up those virtues because their ego told them to. It wants to be ethically superior to other people. But empathy and compassion are not virtues to adopt. They are byproducts of understand that you exist in this existence. And as a part of this existence you have suffered. And you begin to realize there are other people in this same existence that are suffering. So you begin to have empathy for them. And then you realize you should treat people well because they haven't figured out what this existence is that they live in like you might have. Nor have they figured out that they are still prisoners of their own minds.

Without depth of understanding that comes from direct experience, empathy and compassion as adopted virtues are hollow.

Eliminate the judgments: If you've ever lived on this planet anytime during your life you've probably heard "don't be so quick to judge people" or other comments about judging people. But do you really know what this means? I mean REALLY know? When we are thinking of people judging people we often imagine a person talking behind someone's back about their life choices. And we say yourselves "at least I'm not like that". Did you catch it? The judgment that creeped in. Do you you see how sneaky it actually is? Well, it's much sneakier than most people could ever guess.

If you have been practicing a spiritual practice for any significant time then you probably know about the "ego" and the "inner voice". This inner voice, the thing inside your head that keeps giving a play by play narrative of your life, just won't be quiet. It's rare if a person can successful meditate their inner voice away permanently.

I have experienced it, but it only lasted 3 days. I still had to learn to watch my thoughts and develop good internal observation and habits. So here's where the ego becomes the judge in a very sneaky way.

Look at something. Anything. A chair, a tree, a flower, whatever. As soon as your mind starts talking about it, it's labeling. If you look at a flower it might say "that's beautiful". Look at a cute little puppy and it will say "that's cute!". Look at a person with a huge red birthmark on their face and it might say "Oh my God! Poor girl. I'm glad I don't have to live with that."...................................

Let that sink in. Judgment moves at the speed of thought.

So what do you do? Practice looking at something and not letting your inner voice say anything. And if you catch your inner voice labeling anything then practice looking without inner talking. It's hard at first. But it gets easier. Learn to see things exactly as they are. No dialog needed.

POSITIVE MIND REALITY. NEGATIVE MIND REALITY:

Have you ever met someone who was extremely negative? And bad things always happened to them. Every time they get a leg up something comes along and knocks them down. They even begin to expect it. They think that God, or the universe is out to get them or hates them. And the cycle continues.

But, have you ever met someone that is stupidly positive? Every day is a good day to them. Nothing bad ever seems to stick to them. Good things always seem to happen to them. Like life is just on autopilot for them. Things that they want or need just seem to materialize. Like someone gives them a car, or they win a shopping spree.

This is the old saying that *life is a reflection of what you are inside.* It's also manifesting. The more positive you are and the quicker you let the negative things go the better your reality becomes. You begin to realize there are no bad days. Just days when something bad might happen. It's how you react to it that matters.

As I transitioned from being a negative minded person to being a positive minded person through mental training I found my reality changing around me. And the more it changed the more I believed. Then one day I woke up and I knew the truth of it.

So if you are not mindful of your thoughts and you don't stay in the positive you could be manifesting bad things into your life.

POSITIVE AND NEGATIVE DO *NOT* ATTRACT

In the world of science we're told that positive and negative attract. We can see it in effect with iron based metals and magnets. But in the spiritual world it's the opposite. Positive pushes negative away. You may have seen this in your life before. A very positive person comes around a negative person and the negative person whines, complains, maybe tries to get the person fired or removed, even tries to sabotage them. But if the positive person manages to stick through that then the negative person ends up leaving. I've seen it personally in my life many times.

You may have even seen it with shady or dishonest people. A positive person comes around and the dishonest / shady person starts talking bad about them, even tries to turn people against them. One of the most common thing I hear from those negative people is "I don't know what it is about that person, but I don't like them". Even they don't know why they dislike being around a positive person. And they will think that you are shady. This is them projecting their own negative traits out onto their perceived view of the world.

Some people haven't "chosen" which way they are going. They have qualities of both a positive and negative person. And they can be dragged either direction by the people they spend time around. And people that are "negative polarity" have their ethics reversed. They will think it's okay to lie, cheat, steal or do whatever in order to gain whatever they want. They justify it. Even if you flat out catch them they still find a way to justify it, and they are not sorry. Because that is the nature of negative polarity people.

So if you have decided to live the positive life, don't be surprised if you find people that you once hang out with begin to avoid you. You no longer share the same energy. The absolute best thing you can do to "combat" a negative person is to share your positivity all around you, even if they attack you. They will either begin to tune to your positive frequency and change or they will see their way out of your life. I've seen this more than once before.

So stay positive.

SERVICE TO SELF DISGUISED AS SERVICE TO OTHERS:

In the spiritual world sometimes you hear the term service to self and service to others. It's pretty obvious what they are about. But...... There is a spiritual trap in this waiting to snare people.

To truly understand what service to others is you have to truly know what you are..... and aren't. The ability to get out of the prison of the mind and live clearly allows us to understand the suffering that others go through. It is absolutely important to have this deep understanding of the suffering of other people. Because with it we can help other people for the right reasons.

Without it what you will see are people who will say "I want to heal others. I want to help others. I want this or that. I WANT, I WANT, I WANT".

You see, the ego is the real devil inside people. It will hijack your spiritual path in order to make itself feel good. It's the problem you see on videos where people record themselves giving money to homeless people. And it will absolutely take over your life and disguise itself under the flag of "I'm helping people".

But it's not coming from a genuine place. The ego wants something out of it. Only when you truly understand this can you begin to understand what it means to truly serve others...... with no expectations of getting anything out of it.
Go through the gateless gate. Seek first the kingdom of heaven. Realize what you are and are not. Then service to others becomes a natural byproduct of genuine spiritual living.

If you seek mysticism and power first you may gain it. But there are a lot of miserable mystical people out there with serious personal issues. Life will show you who is genuinely walking an enlightened life. If a person is surrounded in chaos and resistance they are most likely not.

WE'RE NOT TRYING TO ACHIEVE AN EMOTIONLESS STATE:

That would be a horrible existence. I know because I've felt that before. But sensations in the body, like anxiety, fear, etc. They have a place. Negative emotions are like the lights on a car dashboard. It doesn't mean your car is broke. It just means you need to pay attention to what is going on because something may be having a negative affect on the car (or your body in this case).

I sometimes face situations where I'm in danger. I have in the past due to my job. And I'm calm when I'm faced with it. But I still feel sensations telling me I need to be careful and aware. I'm just not giving in to the unnecessary fear of the mind.

LETTING GO THEN GRASPING AGAIN. THE MIND TRYING TO CONTROL:

If you have gotten past the basics of understanding the mind, how it causes suffering and how you can be happy then you may have moved into actually living in this existence. You're beginning to understand deeper aspects of life that you may not be able to put into words. You may have seen that letting go of anything brings peace and good things begin to happen. You may be on the verge of trusting life, the universe, God, whatever you want to call it. Maybe you even THINK you trust it. And then this happens. You let go, give into life. You're doing well, maybe even happy. And on that letting go good things begin to happen. Maybe something you have wanted manifests into your life. Then boom. Your mind now wants more. It thinks it knows the trick to how to get more. And it grasps for control again. Then everything that seemed to be going so smoothly stops.

This is normal. It's a part of your evolution. The letting go of control part that you achieved IS the trick to life. But the mind can't stand not having control or the ability to direct effort towards something. So here's the real secret. Become "outcome independent". If you can live your life without caring whether or not you get what your mind wants then you enter the flow state. You have to be good with life no matter what the outcome is. Then if something you've wanted comes along it's just the cherry on top.

True spiritual living is surrender. Acceptance of what is and what will be. Enter into that place and you will live an amazing existence in your body.

YOU ARE LOSING INTEREST IN THINGS YOU ONCE LIKED:

Sometimes, when a person has been able to see what their mind is and what it does, they begin to lose interest in the things they once liked. The reason behind this is because you see through the illusion of your ego. The person you once thought you were is just a creation of the mind. A story you told yourself and other people. I went through it. I used to dream of being a master firearms instructor. I used to lift weights. I hung out with people that talked about guns and tactics. That was my thing. But as I saw my mind my motivation began to dry up. I realized the only reason I wanted to do those things is because I wanted people to think I was "that badass guy".

I was in competition with other people and even myself. Then I got to a point where I didn't know who I was anymore. I didn't know what I liked. I felt lost. Sometime later I was invited to go mountain bike riding with a couple of guys. I had never been so I agreed. I was immediately hooked. I enjoyed it. I liked it, not because I wanted to prove anything to those guys, but because I actually, genuinely enjoyed it. I got my own bike, planned my own trips and still do. Then that branched out into hiking and camping. I began to live. Not to satisfy someone else's ideas of what life is supposed to be. Not for bragging rights. But because I loved it and I felt free. I still don't know who I am (I know what I am though) but that's okay. Because I am. I exist. I am here. I have no one to compete with. And so it will be for you too if you experience the emptiness of not knowing who you are anymore. It's okay. It's normal. And it's an indicator of where you are on the path.

(self realization can occur at any point in life)

ALL BELIEFS ARE LAYERS OF CONDITIONING:

If you look at the world today you will see what appears to be hell. People feel like there are good guys and bad guys, us versus them, my political party is better than your political party, I want you to do what I feel is right and you want me to do what you feel is right, etc. So let's look at a story to see what all of this is.

Let's imagine that one day at the same time around the world everybody just freezers for a second. And during that freeze everybody has their mind wiped of all knowledge except for the ability to talk, clean themselves, eat and the basic functions of living. And all written documentation disappears to, so no books, no history, no records. With no learned beliefs, what would happen? Well, without certain reference points to the past things would get very interesting.

* All victims of all kinds of abuse would have no memory of those wrongs. So a person who had previously been a victim would not be a victim anymore. They would be starting fresh.
* With no memory of the past, racism would instantly vanish. No abusers, no victims. Because without carrying on the memory of racism with its conditioning on both sides it simply disappears.
* All political beliefs disappear. There would be no left, no right. No perceived right or wrong. Just people with no basis to hate each other.
* Moral and ethical codes would be erased. What people think of as right and wrong would be reduced to direct experience that would have to be learned again. And essentially it would come down to the Golden Rule. I don't want to be treated badly. So I won't treat you badly.

Interesting story. Interesting theory. There are ways to test them, and they have been conducted with similar results. Such as children of different races being put in the same rooms together with no learned versions of race history. And they had a grand old time playing together.

So what does this mean for you? It means that everything you hold as a personal code, morals, right, wrong, victims, abusers, political beliefs and more are a part of your conditioned layers of ego. Many, many people get into "spirituality" and try and bring their personal beliefs with them. They try and form spirituality into what they see as the right way. In other words, they put on a "spiritual ego" (the absolute worst ego of all) and judge you inside their head. Or bash people on social media if they don't share the same political view points.

I've seen it said over and over again by spiritual teachers all over the world from all eras. If you want to find the truth you have to give up everything. But only everything. No exceptions. So, are you just dabbling in spirituality to make yourself feel morally superior? Or are you really walking the path and living it?

LEAVE A WAKE. AFFECT THE WORLD WITH YOUR ENERGY:

One day I came to a bit of understanding that was deeper than normal. Of course that depth may be lost in this writing, but I'm sure it will find a place in someone's mind when they need it.

As we travel through this life we leave a wake behind us. Like a boat. Everything we do, positive and negative, casts a wave on the other boats around us. As we journey we may make mistakes. Sometimes it's something we do that may be hurtful to someone else.

When you recognize that, do your best to reel in your ego and continue to refine the spirit. And forgive yourself. Just do your best to not continue making the same mistakes. But also realize that sometimes grit is needed to polish stones.

When you do something negative it may have been needed to ignite something in someone else. Don't use this as an excuse to do bad things, just realize that in the bigger scheme of things, our abrasive actions may have been caused by something higher than us for a purpose.

As you continue to refine the spirit you can look back and see the positive changes you've had on those people you've left in your wake. Eventually your wake won't capsize other boats, but will gently rock them, causing the passengers to smile and wave.

LOGIC VERSUS QUANTUM FEELING:

As some of you may have noticed you get to a point where logic fails. You can only think so much about something and can only understand it to the limits of your brain. And you may have experienced the ability to relax the mind, let go of trying to mentally grasp something and then you experience a whole new level. It's like thinking, but without the thinking. You come to experience things, reach understandings or even instantaneous "knowing" of something.

Scientists have found that our brains are able to compute in something like 11 dimensions. Which means we literally have a quantum computer in our skulls. And to use it you can't try and control it. This is how you can have a topic in the back of your mind and the answer comes to you in some form or another. It could be days or weeks. But the answer comes. This is also where you gain the ability to trust life itself and know that everything is going to be fine.

BEWARE THE EGO TRAP OF THE *DIVINE MISSION:*

Often, through understanding of our own suffering we gain a desire to help people. Helping people is noble and good. But if we want to move in harmony with life itself there needs to be some deeper realizations. These realizations will allow for a better, more efficient way to help people.

In spiritual practice there's a lot of emphasis on understanding the mind and it's traps. Ego / mind will use anything it can against you in order to maintain control. It will even use your passions and personal codes and ethics against you. One very sneaky form of ego that causes people to become stagnant in their spiritual development and understanding is something I refer to as "the divine mission". It uses a person's own desires to help people as a driving force. There's nothing wrong with wanting to help people. But let's go through some basic truths.

Suffering existed before you were born. It will exist after you die. You do not fail by not helping everybody. It's physically impossible in this form to help everybody.

You can't chase people in order to get them to change. Modern Christian church chases people, uses judgments, guilt, shame and more in order to get people to do what they want them to do in the name of trying to *save them* from eternal suffering. It's not effective in this modern world. It was effective when the churches with the power of kings and armies behind them forced people through violence and death. But we all know there's nothing godly about that. But do not use this as ammo against those good, very deeply spiritual people that are living the words of Yeshua. There are some amazing Christians who truly live with love in their hearts towards everyone.

You can't help someone that doesn't want to be helped. Badgering them makes them run away from you faster. Every person has to actively choose to change and then we can help them by just being available when it's wanted. We also have to change who we are inside. By doing this and moving in harmony through life we become a magnet for those who are seeking, even if they don't know they are seeking.

Deep realizations of what our "reality", God, the universe, whatever you want to call it, shows us that it is an interactive, highly intelligent sentience that is far wiser than we could be in this form. By thinking we know better we are not trusting it. People misunderstand suffering. Suffering is the catalyst for change. We label things as good, bad, evil, divine, not understanding that it all works together for its own purposes. Even evil has a purpose, though it may not be readily seen for what it is. A bad thing you did to someone in the past may have been the necessary push that got them to turn fully to the light by realizing they don't want to treat people that way.

Then there's the issue of work load. Could you talk to a person for two hours on the phone each day? What about 3 people for two hours each? What about 10 people? 1,000? When do you realize that you can't save the world by yourself?

In Daoism there is something called Wu Wei. It loosely translates to "do without doing". By changing ourselves and our energy, making ourselves available to the creative forces that make everything possible, we become an instrument to help others. We move when it's time to move. Other people come to us. We don't chase them. And they are already receptive to whatever we have to show them. And we show them with our own lives. We become a living embodiment of the love and compassion that people so desperately seek. Without judgment. Without trying to convince them like a used car salesman. And with the willingness to help them when they are ready. Not because "I want" them to be ready.

In this way, life sorts those who are ready and our efforts become more efficient. It arranges the meeting for us and gives us the time to do what needs to be done. We can only do so much. But we can do a lot by just trusting in this life if we can put our own minds to the side.

INTERESTING PERSONAL STORY ABOUT FEELING EMOTIONS:

I was admin and field operations where I used to work. One day I get a call from a guy that worked under me and he starts listing reasons why he can't do a certain thing. But I know the guy. I know that he plays games in order to get favorable situations at work. And the excuse he gives me over the phone for this particular something was just grasping for straws to get out of where he was working because he was bored.

So because I have a decent level of separation between my ego and my consciousness I have to put on masks to be able to do my job. The world expects you to be a certain way while doing certain things. So instead of being some super spiritual, mantra chanting monk at work I have to become the boss necessary to do the job. So I get there, slip into the necessary character, deal with the guy and his issue and then drive home.

Well, even when you know what your mind is doing your body still has that mind / body connection. So I'm driving home and I can feel the emotion in my chest. It's the irritated, aggrevated, slightly angry feeling most people experience when they know a person has stolen from them and they know the person personally. (say that five times fast). But I know where my mind is at. Mentally I'm cool as a cucumber. But my body is apparently still enjoying the show.

So I turn my focus to it and something strange happened. I was detached from the physical emotion in my chest so I was seeing it in my mind almost third person view. And I was ENJOYING it. It was exciting. It's like listening to an angry rock song a person would listen to while at the gym in order to motivate themselves. So I listened for a while and enjoyed the experience of it just being there.

Moral of the story. There are many levels and indicators along the way that you are making progress. Don't forget to enjoy the process instead of just trying to skip to the end.

GENUINE DEEP PERSONAL WORK TO ACHIEVE PEACE:

The quote listed below has to do with minds of people. So many people think that we need to achieve this or that or DO something to bring peace. But people don't understand that the evil they see in this world is really from inside of them. If you look at a person with a different political view and you wish harm on them, even inside of your own head, that's evil. If you hate Christians because of how they behave, that's evil. Evil is the despicable thoughts that run through your mind, sometimes leading to despicable actions. Are you really a practicing "spiritual" person? Or are you a fraud that drapes themselves in the appearance of being spiritual while merely adopting some spiritual traits and not deeply knowing why those traits should be followed?

"We often think of peace as the absence of war, that if powerful countries would reduce their weapon arsenals, we could have peace. But if we look deeply into the weapons, we see our own minds- our own prejudices, fears and ignorance.

Even if we transport all the bombs to the moon, the roots of war and the roots of bombs are still there, in our hearts and minds, and sooner or later we will make new bombs.

To work for peace is to uproot war from ourselves and from the hearts of men and women. To prepare for war, to give millions of men and women the opportunity to practice killing day and night in their hearts, is to plant millions of seeds of violence, anger, frustration, and fear that will be passed on for generations to come. "

~Thich Nhat Hanh

FOR THE SEEKER, THE ANSWERS WILL COME:

One of the thoughts I have periodically is "Why couldn't I have found out what I know now back when I was 20? Life would have been so much easier."
The answer is that I didn't have the right mindset needed to grasp many of these concepts. Unfortunately and fortunately (figure that one out) my personal suffering was the catalyst necessary to push me to the point where I was willing to try anything to get life to stop being so hard. Which leads to the next thought. "If I had done 'this' at this time I would have learned all this quicker and more efficiently.". But again, everything comes to you at the moment in time when you are ready for that piece of information or motivation.

One of the hardest concepts to understand is that the life we live in, the reality, the universe, whatever you want to call it, is actually listening to you. And often it is also trying to communicate with you. This energy field we call life will answer your questions. It may not be as simple as a phone call from God, but it could be a commercial on TV, a random video on the internet, a post on Facebook, etc.
But more often than not most people are just not paying attention. We may call it synchronicity or coincidence.

But that's just the ego's way of trying to discredit your lived experience.

Apparently I was hard headed when I entered this world of spiritual practice. I wouldn't pay attention unless I saw something 3 times. So life adapted to my learning patterns and began dropping 3 clues back to back to back on me which got my attention a lot quicker. Now when I have a question I just keep my eyes open. The answer usually comes quickly and it doesn't have to hit me with multiple clues.

How does this apply to you? You have questions. Life has answers. Start paying attention. It will drop the answers into your field of view. You just need to be receptive.
Want to know what is like to live a mystical experience? Start listening to life.

FUNNY STORY ABOUT EGO:

Story written by Pierre Will (I give credit where credit is due)

Su Dongpo (蘇東坡) was an avid student of Buddhist teachings and a distinguished and mischievous poet. He was quick-witted and humorous; as a Zen Buddhist follower he was very serious and self-disciplined. He often discussed Buddhism with his good friend, Zen Master Fo Yin (佛印禪師). The two lived across the river from one another.

Following is an interesting and famous story about him and Zen Master Fo Yin.
One day, Su Dongpo felt inspired and wrote the following poem :

稽首天中天， (Qǐshǒu tiān zhōng tiān),
毫光照大千； (Háo guāngzhào dàqiān);
八風吹不動， (Bā fēngchuī bùdòng),
端坐紫金蓮。 (Duān zuò zǐjīn lián).
I bow my head to the heaven within heaven,
Hairline rays illuminating the universe,
The eight winds cannot move me,
Sitting still upon the purple golden lotus.

The "eight winds" (八風) in the poem referred to praise (稱), ridicule (譏), honor (譽), disgrace (毀), gain (得), loss (失), pleasure (樂) and misery (苦) – interpersonal forces of the material world that drive and influence the hearts of men. Su Dongpo was saying that he has attained a higher level of spirituality, where these forces no longer affect him.
Impressed by himself, Su Dongpo sent a servant to hand-carry this poem to Fo Yin. that his friend would be equally impressed. When Fo Yin read the poem, he immediately saw that it was both a tribute to the Buddha and a declaration of spiritual refinement. Smiling, the Zen Master wrote "fart" on the manuscript and had it returned to Su Dongpo.

Su Dongpo was expecting compliments and a seal of approval. When he saw "fart" written on the manuscript, he was shocked . He burst into anger: "How dare he insult me like this ? Why that lousy old monk ! He's got a lot of explaining to do !"

Full of indignation, he rushed out of his house and ordered a boat to ferry him to the other shore as quickly as possible. He wanted to find Fo Yin and demand an apology. However, Fo Yin's door closed. On the door was a piece of paper, for Su Dongpo. The paper had following two lines :

八風吹不動，
一屁彈過江。

The eight winds cannot move me,
One fart blows me across the river.

This stopped Su Dongpo cold. Fo Yin had anticipated this hot-headed visit. Su Dongpo's anger suddenly drained away as he understood his friend's meaning. If he really was a man of spiritual refinement, completely unaffected by the eight winds, then how could he be so easily provoked ?

With a few strokes of the pen and minimal effort, Fo Yin showed that Su Dongpo was in fact not as spiritually advanced as he claimed to be. Ashamed but wiser, Su Dongpo departed quietly.

This event proved to be a turning point in Su Dongpo's spiritual development. From that point on, he became a man of humility, and not merely someone who boasted of possessing the virtue.

Zen is a state of mind, a level of awareness, a way of life. Zen that focuses on the meaning and games of words is a formal and courtly Zen and cultic Zen. Zen like that has no correlation with the true Zen.

THE DARK NIGHT OF THE SOUL:

For those of you who may have started walking a spiritual path or meditation there is a condition that arises for most people referred to as the dark night of the soul. I'll do my best to explain it and please feel free to share your story as it may help others.

When we first begin a spiritual practice we may have a bunch of realizations come to us quickly. One of those realizations being that our ego, our persona, the voice inside of our head is not us. We can't get it to shut up permanently, it's always trying to drag you into drama and scenarios that make you feel bad and it's almost always negative. What ends up happening is that this ego, this active uncontrollable mind realizes that you have started practices that will eventually free you from its control. And so the ego begins to use every trick it knows to need with you and get you to abandon your spiritual practice. And one of those ways is experienced as the Dark Night of the Soul.

During the dark night of the soul you may experience worthlessness, fear, lack of motivation, depression, anxiety, that nothing matters. And it is relentless. But there's good news. If you keep your practice up and especially continue to do ego work then you will come out of the dark night of the soul.

My dark night of the soul was terrifying. I used to have a form of PTSD that caused me not to feel much in the way of emotions. Except for anger. I felt that a lot. As my realizations of what my ego was began to sink in and I could see the motives of my mind more clearly I began to fear death. I mean REALLY fear it. I had never really thought about death but all of a sudden it really bothered me. To the point where I was thinking about dying every day for six + months. So instead of running from it I dove into the ideas of death and what happens after life as we know it. I spent months contemplating death. Until one day I became good with death. My mind had taken me through every scenario of how I could die, what happened to my consciousness, all the people I would leave behind and more.

Eventually I came to accept it and become comfortable with it. And then I was out of the dark night of the soul. And once my fear of death was over life got much easier. Once you lose the fear of death what else can bother you?

Everyone may experience the dark night of the soul differently. But there seems to be common threads among them.

Wu Wei. It comes from eastern enlightenment practices of China called Daoism. It means effortless action or to do without doing. Or as I call it, effortless living. When you enter the flow state of life itself, everything you need is provided. But how can a person achieve effortless living? Here's a basic way to achieve it.

1. Stay positive using the mental exercises that reinforce natural positive mental states.

2. Accept EVERYTHING as it is. When something bad happens, don't label it as bad because it reinforces it. Just see it, then move on and stay positive.

3. Do without doing. Just exist as a form of observing. Watch as what you need materializes without having to do anything. With a positive mind, you expect things to be positive so reality creates it in your mental image.

Whatever you expect to happen happens. So if you are negative minded and expect bad things, bad things will happen.

SELF SABOTAGE. A TRULY DIABOLICAL TRAIT OF EGO:

In the past I have seen people dealing with a different kind of problem that ego can create. Self sabotage. When we are studying the mind, the ego, in order to realize how many problems it creates for us, we often only see the obvious signs of it. The inner voice. The inner voice is the easiest part of the ego to see. But that's just the first level of ego. The second level of ego is less obvious. It's the scenarios your mind creates, your belief systems, your personal values, your passions and dislikes, etc. After you begin to see the ego's most obviously form, which is the inner voice, then it begins to shift tactics in order to stay in control of you. And while I've seen self sabotage before it didn't click for me the way it has recently since I've seen two people I know get stuck in it without any awareness of it.

Self sabotage is a form of self degradation. The inner voice may have been obvious in it's attacks on you by saying you're not worthy of good things, putting you down, being negative, causing you to doubt yourself, etc. But self sabotage is even sneakier. Usually a person who self sabotages themselves has had a lot of bad things happen in life or were verbally or mentally abused and degraded. So what happens is when things start to go right in life and everything is running smoothly, something inside of them begins to look for the bad thing it is expecting to show up. And sometimes, instead of waiting for something bad to happen, it creates something bad. It creates drama, or begins to detach from people in anticipation of its fear of abandonment, creates unnecessary conflicts with people over things that don't matter, etc.

The mind has experienced so much negativity that it thinks it's normal. And when things are going right it becomes suspicious of it. I've heard it said before that "peace feels like boredom to people who are used to chaos". My own mother couldn't handle peace. When things were going right she would pick a fight, or begin planning to move or get another job.

If you detect this pattern inside of yourself and feel you're on the verge of creating unnecessary conflict, then take the time to put yourself in a positive frame of mind and just wait it out. After you've established a good record of peace then the mind begins to see that there are other possibilities than expecting negativity.

TRUE TOXIC POSITIVITY:

Believe it or not there is such a thing as toxic positivity. Although many people don't really understand what it is.

Life is filled with all kinds of energy. Positive, negative and a whole spectrum of everything in between. Toxic positivity is the action of trying to keep everything positive in *appearance* by rejecting anything with an appearance of being negative or by bombarding the person or area with "love, light and good vibes". The problem is that life is not all roses and sunshine for everyone at any given time. If you attempt to avoid the negative in life you are avoiding life itself.

Life and spirituality are not just one big hunky dory party. You are going to have negative emotions and reactions to life. We are not trying to create an impossible utopia of positive energy. We learn to just accept whatever happens in life, including the bad. What our minds perceive as bad may just be a perspective as another person may not see it as bad. But our bodies may have a physical reaction to something, such as a fear that arises in certain situations. Or if we grieve the loss of a loved one.

If you find a group or a person who doesn't allow talk of negative situations in life in order to help find a solution and all they want to do is mask everything with this fake positivity in order to hide what's really going on and avoid the truth, then that is toxic. A truly deep spiritual person knows that their mind is the cause of suffering and they control what they think about in order to reduce or eliminate unnecessary suffering. But we are still in this life and life is not always pleasant. And a person who can be genuine with their emotions can help other people when they are going through hard times.

FINDING DIVINITY:

Along your path of self discovery and your practice you may begin to have experiences. Some of them can be quite profound. As you begin to see through your mind you can begin to experience Life. The real life. The living entity that we are all a part of. And you may sense a great sense of intelligence coming from it. A part of you spiritual practice is to spend time meditating. Not just because it's good for you, but because it will help you *see* in a very different way. And eventually you will find out the truth. I will not go into much detail about my direct experience as it will taint your ability to see without bias. But you will have your own experiences and understanding that will change life for you permanently.

LIVE YOUR LIFE:

There's a very subtle ego trap that can arise in people. After they've had their deep realizations they get caught in this loop of seeking more and more. Once you've realized your mind and eventually yourself and reality, then go and live your life.

I once had a lady tell me she doesn't engage in small talk (can you feel the judgement in that sentence?). She only wants to talk about spirituality and mysticism. Think about this. "I want" and "I don't want" are ego.

And not being available to other people in your life in a way they can understand is really selfish. I can't expect a person at a gas station to be able to understand what I know. And I wouldn't expect them to nor would I push my knowledge on them. If they want to talk about their day or their dog or their grandchildren then I will make myself available for that. If you mind only wants to talk about spirituality and mysticism then you aren't truly free from it. It's attempting to collect information in order to control it. And you. No amount of information will ever satisfy the mind. It always wants more.

And this is the reason that I rarely read books that people suggest to me. Life itself brings me information exactly when I need it. I don't usually have to search for it. So instead of packing my brain full of information that may or may not be true in someone else's view of life, I just allow life to be. I am not opposed to other people's views of spirituality. I just know that there's a million flavors of ice cream and they are all made in similar ways. I don't need to taste all of them. I have read enough of other people's material to know that we are all talking about the same thing, just using different words or concepts to achieve the same goal.

DON'T DISMISS YOUR EXPERIENCE:

I used to go around listening to other peoples' spiritual experiences and comparing myself. The problem was that my experiences didn't accurately match theirs. And so I would brush off my own experiences. Later on I would have a realization that I had a certain experience. One of the big experiences I had was a kundalini awakening. I just brushed it off as a weird occurrence. But I didn't realize that what had happened was actually a pretty big deal. All because I was looking and wanting other people's experiences.

Don't chase other people's experiences. Pay attention to your own life and experiences. Don't brush anything off without truly analyzing it. Some of the deepest experiences in life can only be felt by feeling for the subtle. Meditation in particular requires a feel for the subtle. Not every experience is going to be big and magical with dragons and fireworks.

The day I realized that a creative force that we may call God exists, I realized it at the same way that I knew that I was wearing pants. If you ask yourself, am I wearing pants and the answer is yes.......that's it. No big fireworks show. It simply *is*. And that realization then hit me like a lightning bolt through my spine. It wasn't amazing because of a big magical experience. It was amazing because there wasn't a big magical experience and the *knowing* just hit me. It was as if I had always known. There was no wandering thoughts and doubt trying to examine it. It was just simple truth experienced simply.

DON'T CHASE PEOPLE TO CHANGE THEM:

On our spiritual journey we will be tempted to chase people. We may want to have them experience what we experience in order to help them. And if you do you're going to come off as a spiritual zealot. Kind of like door to door religious people trying to convert you. A person is only ready when they are ready. If you truly want to help people, change yourself first. Get into the flow of life. Be happy and unshakable. Cultivate a life that even if you lived *in a van down by the river* that other people will be envious of your happiness. This will bring questions. And then you can answer their questions. But make sure that you keep your mind in check that it doesn't begin to reach again.

If you burn a person out while chasing them with spirituality then you will create bigger walls inside of them and they will be harder to help in the future.

DON'T AUTO LABEL ANYTHING:

You may notice that as you walk around in life your mind will see something and say it's label. You may see a flower and your inner voice may say "flower" or "beautiful". Try and practice seeing without the inner voice labeling. The better you get at this the better you will become at taking in life. You will be a better active listening for other people, you'll stop making snap judgments about people you see, and you'll be able to see clues that life brings you.

MEMORIES COME BACK TO LIFE:

In the first first years of your spiritual practice you may notice that you have a lot of memories coming up from the past. Things that may seem absolutely mundane or even meaningless. You may have a memory of the time you were 5 riding a big wheel trike through the neighborhood with other kids. These memories coming up are a natural part of spirituality. As you get older the random memories popping up will become fewer and far between. Some memories may be something that you never came to terms with. And some may be just random bits of data the subconscious is reorganizing.

BE OPEN:

A part of evolving on our spiritual path is being open to possibility. Many times our minds will tell us that something isn't possible. Maybe it is, maybe it isn't. But…...how do you *know*? If your mind automatically places judgments on things or concepts without you directly experiencing it then you may stop yourself from even trying. It's like how guys who may not be super attractive on the social appearance scale can have a very attractive girlfriend. Other guys may be too intimidated to talk to the woman because they feel she will only be attracted to guys you see on fitness magazines. How do you know she's in a relationship or not interested in you unless you take the chance to find out?

It's the same way in our lives with literally everything. So if you catch your mind creating doubt or trying to *protect* you from embarrassing yourself, then realize that's just the problem solving part of your ego trying to prevent you from harm.

EXPECTATIONS:

Having expectations is the fastest way to disappointment and is a condition of the ego. We can expect other people to behave a certain way. We can expect our job to be run by ethical management. But in life our own expectations create inner strife. If you can go into life with no expectations then you won't really face any disappointments. You won't be worried about things either. And this is definitely a good way to stay centered and peaceful.

SEPARATING EMOTIONS FROM SENSATIONS:

Sometimes our body needs to communicate something to us. It could be an illness, an injury, a problem that your subconscious sees but you haven't seen yet. And it's not like your body or subconscious has a cell phone and can contact you directly and say "Hey man, we've got an issue that needs your attention.".

So our body may experience emotions. It could be in the form of depression or anxiety or something else. If you know that you are in a good place mentally and have no reason to have depression or anxiety or whatever emotion you're feeling, then pay attention to what's going on around you. And it's possible that there's really nothing wrong going on. Your body just may be having a weird chemical day. You could have eaten something that your meat suit (body) doesn't like. Just realize that the feeling will go away.

Use every sensation in your body, including your emotions, as a form of radar into what's going on with you. These are tools. Don't be afraid of emotions.

THE INBETWEEN:

In meditation as well as in life there is a place that is hard to find at first. In between one thought and another. In between sounds. In between. Some call it the void. Some call it nothingness. It's where you don't see or detect anything with normal senses. But if you focus on this place you begin to get a sense that there's something there. And this something is literally everywhere. In everything. You get a sense there's an intelligence. Something that goes well beyond the concept of ancient. And extremely potent. If or when you start to sense this then spend time here. There's a deepness here that will bring more with it. It's so hard to talk about this without trying to go into concepts. Because really you can't. You know there's something here but it can't be put into words because………..there's nothing there. Yet there is. Spend time here if you can. The faster you find it and the more time you spend here the better.

THE INNER GURU:

There is a saying that says "When the student is ready the teacher appears. When the student is truly ready the teacher disappears."

I have spent a lot of my time being alone in my spiritual journey. Yet I have always had those I have considered mentors to guide me. I have watched life bring me answers almost as if it's listening. Because it is. This reality we live in is extremely responsive to you. That's why it's so important to understand that what you think about is important. Never wish bad on people as it creates situations. Always wish well and bless people. Always have gratitude. Never worry about what you don't have. Let love and compassion flow from you to everyone and everything. To pay attention to the inner guru is to pay attention to life itself. Ask a question. And watch as answers come. Don't limit the answers to only one way, such as God making a phone call to you. The answers can come in any form. From any place. And don't worry about missing the message. Your own awareness will be drawn to it. All you have to do is trust life itself. Stay in the flow state with it. Keep your mind at bay as much as you can and just *feel* life move.

TRUSTING LIFE:

Once you've been on the path a while and you've gotten comfortable with it. Once you've had deep realizations about your mind, about the core of what you are, about reality itself, there comes a sense of trust. You've watched life move around you. Provide you with everything you need. You've seen things that science has a hard time explaining. You've watched how you affect others simply by existing in their presence. You've watched as bad situations were met with solutions shortly afterwards with little effort on your part, almost miraculously. So you begin to trust life.

Trusting life brings another level of existence. You don't worry about much. You're compassionate and empathetic to others around you at a level you never thought imaginable. You recognize that you are a part of life itself as such it will move you in place to help other people. Whether you are aware of life moving you or not you are being moved. Everything you do matters. There are no coincidences. One life flows into another. It's the butterfly effect in action. And you know there is no separateness between you and anything else in this creation we exist in. You don't fear death the way you once did. It even gets to a point where you don't view death the traditional way either. You begin to perceive it as just moving into another level of existence.

This is where the deep learning begins. This is where you become a student of life itself. And your experiences will become stories and lessons to help other people while refining your spirit for whatever evolutionary process you are going through.

A CHOICE TO BE MADE:

Realization of life. Of it's movements and how you exist within it. The trust you develop for it. Eventually there's a choice that a person can be faced with. To accept it and move with it, which will lead you to help other people. Or to move only for yourself, choosing a selfish life of "I want".

I have watched this occur with people. Those who have seen the miracles of life itself and then decide to follow their own wants and desires seem to have a retraction of the benefits they were once blessed with. They exist, but the drama and other issues seem to return. They cease to evolve further into spirituality, eventually coming to believe there's nothing left and they know everything they need to know. And suffering even returns. They can even become filled with negative ego and treat other people as inferior. Their development on the path seems to stop as they are no longer flowing with life but choosing to satisfy themselves first. Believing that they will somehow get what they need later in life once they get older and no longer have the same desires. Maybe it's true. Maybe it's not. But watching life get harder or fall back to the old ways with people seems to be an indicator to me that the choice to serve themselves is not good.

There are some people who never make a choice. Never dedicate themselves to life and what it wants. They seem to fall into some sort of living purgatory. They exist but not necessarily happy. Because they have seen the amazing movements of life and tasted freedom of their mind for a while. And once you see something you can't unsee it. So they know there's more out there but are stuck in their old lives. Never committing to moving further down the spiritual path. I have even seen someone I know personally make the statement that he would choose later in life as he's got things he wants to do first.

I do not say this as some sort of religious dogma or rule that has to be followed. But after talking with lots of people on the path and watching the evolution that occurs with them this is more of an observation. Life wakes people up when they are ready. There's something ancient and wise there. We seem to have a purpose. To turn our backs on it for selfish reasons seems to set people back. I don't believe it's a punishment. More of an equal amount of effort on both sides. In the end life will still use a person as it needs to for whatever it needs. Now and in the future.

A person who chooses to dedicate their existence to whatever life wants regardless of their own personal desires does so without expectation of reward. And one should never be given an ultimatum to make this choice. Every person I've ever met that has made the choice to dedicate themselves to a spiritual path does so on their own after they have certain realizations.

THE ORIGINS OF THE IDEAS OF GOOD AND EVIL AND THE MORALS THAT HAVE ARISEN:

Morals about good and evil, right and wrong and what people expect from other people is loosely based on two things. The Golden Rule and culture.

The Golden Rule is "Treat others as you would want to be treated." This is also the basis of how we want to exist. Morals based on culture are just how society expects you to behave. And that could be based on numerous factors. Region, religion, race, etc. But to truly break down everything to it's base code of how we get to the concept of right and wrong then the Golden Rule is king. And it's based on our existence. Let's do a thought experiment.

Do you want to be murdered? Tortured? Raped? Stolen from? Your property destroyed? Your family members kidnapped? Your children harmed? Extorted by organized criminals or gangs? Threatened with violence? Threatened with homelessness or poverty? Shamed publicly? Etc.

You exist in this reality. And in this form we are biological creatures that have the capacity to feel severe pain, emotionally and physically. If you look at an animal that has been abused and yet someone took the time to clean them up, feed them, gain their trust, love them and watch as that amazing life blossoms and you see the capacity of the animal to love. This is good. This is godly. This is love.

The basis for all natural morals in our existence is that we don't want bad things to happen to us. And a realization of that is that we shouldn't want to harm others too. People, animals or even the earth we live on.

People have written laws on this. And they exist in every country around the world.

But laws can and have been written that do not benefit society but tilt the playing field to benefit certain people. But there's no point in going over that. It is just a point to be made that not all morals and ethics were made based on the natural morals of existence.

DISCERNMENT:

One of the gifts we are given in this life is the power of discernment. This innate ability for those who are on the spiritual path is something we seem to have been born with. As children we were often sensitive to a lot of things others seemed to ignore. But the power of discernment is an amazing tool that we can use to stay on track or to discover answers. In the Indian tradition of Advaita there is supposedly a set of instructions for how to use it and be able to tell the difference between the mind and what is real. But I'm going to list what my experience has been and it seems to ring true for other people when they directly study it.

We have to go on feel for this. Truth itself has no feel. If I make a statement that "I am breathing air" while keeping my mind quiet and just *feeling* what my mind does, I find that my mind stays quiet. Truth doesn't have a feel because it's already perfect as it is. But if we say something that may be a blatant non truth such as "The Bible was written by God himself, is perfect and was never altered by man"…….there's something inside of us that has this really weird resistance.

We know that the bible has been altered. It wasn't even originally put together until 325 AD at the first council of Nicea that was arranged by emperor Constantine of Rome. We can feel that the different books in the bible were written by men and even Christianity will admit that. God himself didn't come down from the heavens and write different scrolls then bind them into a book. If you can believe the stories, technically the only thing God directly wrote was the ten commandments on stone tablets. If you believe the stories. Stories that were recorded by men. Men who have motives. And if you look around at society today we see what the motives of men is capable of. We know that different books of the bible were removed over the course of the history of the bible. Something around 44 of them were taken out. Yet there are people who claim the bible was written by God himself. When pressed on the matter they will say that the books of the bible were "inspired" by God. But there are also people who believe the earth is only 5000 years old and dinosaur bones were put on the earth to test or challenge Christians' faith.

So for many of us who were raised in ultra religious Christian homes we were told not to question anything, take it all on faith, and trust the people in power who were telling us to believe these things. But for those of us with the power of discernment this doesn't sit well with us. We can *feel* non truth. It doesn't mean what people are doing is evil. And people can believe and spread information they truly believe but is not true. But we have an allergy to non truth. And this allergy was with us all through life. We knew when people were lying to us even if we couldn't prove it. We knew when information was not true even if the person telling it to us actually believed it. And now we can use that tool to feel our way down the spiritual path.

There's a third type of feel that can happen too. It's where there's truth but that truth has depth to it. It almost speaks to us. We find it in writings that somehow catch our attention in ways we can't explain. And it seems like we are supposed to find that information. Almost like it was seeking us. And more often than not the truth that really stands out to us is something very profound that stirs out soul and points us in a direction to look.

But as with all things, be careful of ego. The mind will reach for things it likes or wants. When we feel things without the mind reaching then it's untainted by the mind. So, don't be afraid to question yourself. Make sure it's not something you just want to believe and the mind tricks you into accepting it.

THE VOICELESS VOICE:

Saint Theresa of Avila recorded a lot of her mystical experiences. And one of the things she recorded she called the voiceless voice. It's when *something* suddenly speaks directly to you inside your head. It's not in words yet you understand it clearly as if it was words. And it only speaks once. It never really seems to repeat itself. We can speculate what the voiceless voice is. We can guess that it's our higher selves, God, angels, etc. But those of us who have experienced it can attest that when it happens it's quite profound and strikes us deeply.

Now, be careful that you don't fall prey to ego with this. The difference between the voiceless voice and ego is that ego acts like a used car salesman and does everything in it's power to try and convince you of whatever it's telling you. The voiceless voice usually only speaks once and it moves you deeply. There is a big distinction.

DEATH:

Eventually you will have to come to terms with death if you haven't done it already. We age throughout our lives, gain health and age problems and eventually we graduate from this life into the next existence, whatever that is. If you are a deep person and truly follow your spiritual existence then you will most likely come to good terms with the idea of death and not be afraid of it.

You will see a pattern in life that people who never really thought about spirituality or religion start to get older. And suddenly that guy who was a pretty mean bully in life or was mean or even evil to people suddenly gets religious in old age. It's like they use religion as some sort of insurance for the afterlife.

I find myself fascinated by aging. I look in the mirror and see new lines forming around my eyes. The maturing of my face. I see women walking through the grocery store that are aging with true grace and not allowing it to bother them. There is an absolute beauty to it. And I am not scared of it anymore.

NOT THE BODY. NOT THE MIND:

If you've ever paid attention to any kind of spirituality in your life you may have heard the term "not the body, not the mind". At first it doesn't make sense. Then as you do the ego work you see that you don't actually control the mind. That you are an awareness that is aware of the mind and body. But how do you get to the point where you realize you are not your body?

I have had personal experiences where I could feel the separation between my consciousness and my body. It's very strange to be able to recognize the meat suit, the organism that your body is. And to be aware that it is aware that you see yourself as separate. There's times when my body will respond to stimuli, because it's designed to do that. I can feel the organism, the body get panicked over something it feels threatened by. And yet my mind will be completely calm.

The body also contains the brain. And the brain has the mind, which is the software. But you, the real you, are the consciousness floating around inside your body. Not the body, not the mind. And to experience that is fascinating. And it can give you some compassion for the body as you realize it really is an organism that just wants to stay alive and be happy. It's what is seeking comfort, food and more. There are times when we have to recognize the sensations of the body and tell it that everything is fine and you have interest in seeing it get harmed.

Such an interesting existence we live in.

LIFE IS FASCINATING:

I see everything in life as fascinating now. Even when I'm not doing much and might even be bored, it's still fascinating. I walk through life without fear and I find so much about everything to be interesting. People, interactions, the drama of the world, the petty things that people get amped up over. But more importantly the absolute beauty of this creation we live in. I go backpacking and camping and love to see the trees and waterfalls and lakes and rivers. I love to watch the sunrise and sunsets that I see everyday living in the southwest of the United States in northern New Mexico. Even days where it's rainy and cold and other people let the weather get them down. It's fascinating. So much beauty in everything. I have even found beauty in things that used to scare me. Everything from dark movies and art, music and more. Without the fear I can truly see the beauty even in the darkness.

THE EVIL OF THE GREATER GOOD:

The greater good has been the source of justification of so much evil in this world. People approach life backwards. They don't work on themselves and become amazing loving spirits. Instead they move from ego and decide that in order to make the world a better place things must be done "for the greater good". And they will absolutely justify evil actions to do it. This is how evil uses the passions of people who want to do the right thing in order to twist them into doing bad things.

Look at the Salem witch trials, the crusades, the Spanish inquisition, the justification of slaughter of Natives on all continents in order to take their land. The wars we've seen where soldiers were sent to other countries to "help" those people but in the end it turned out to be a grab for control of resources. People who are easy to bring to high emotional states are easy to manipulate. And the greater good is almost always used by those in power to mobilize the mob mentality in order to achieve their goals.

I am not bashing our military members. I am a veteran myself. I understand that at this point in our existence there are very real threats and someone has to be ready to stand in the way to stop bad things from happening. Even India has a military. And there are Buddhists in the armed forces in the United States. What a lot of people don't realize is that Buddha himself was a trained warrior and battlefield commander. It was expected of all male royalty in that region of the world. And Buddha was a prince of a very powerful king. And the male heirs of kings received the best training in combat and warfare.

So if anyone says that to be a soldier means you can't be spiritual, they obviously don't know the history of Buddha. Buddha knew how to kill other people very effectively and command an army long before he experienced his enlightenment.

SPIRITUAL YEARNING:

Inside of every deep spiritual seeker is something that drives us. It's an unseen force. It's like an itch you can't scratch. And it's why we continue to seek throughout our life. Sure we may stop seeking certain aspects of our existence as realization sets in. But the itch never goes away. If you've ever read Autobiography of a Yogi you will see this drive that all of these amazing spiritual people have through their entire organic lives. And no amount of reading or spiritual practice ever makes it go away. It's the reason why we have a spiritual practice and put in effort every day. For without we would get bored and fall off the path.

FINAL THOUGHTS:

By not being locked in to any particular "style" of eastern spiritual practice I didn't come in with any biases or beliefs. I didn't have the fear of asking people *why* something is done or not done a certain way. I didn't let a sense of loyalty blind me and ignore my own experience and follow the words or beliefs of others unchallenged. My way is my own. The further I go the less structure I use to prop up my spirituality. I don't need to. I watch everything I need appear in life when it's needed. I am not without. Should I spend my life without lots of money and die penniless I will not feel sorry for myself. I love this life and what creates it. I am in awe of it. And I will spend my time on earth helping others put an end to their suffering. If other spiritual lineages and teachers say I am doing it wrong..............then maybe I'll get it right next lifetime.

A person who reads this book may be trying to figure out a starting point for spirituality because they don't know where to start. They may feel stuck and somehow this book finds it's way into their hands and gets them past something that was holding them back. Or maybe it was just something *random* and a person with no spiritual knowledge or even desire to become spiritual somehow stumbles upon this book. There are no coincidences. And I do not endorse or judge one spiritual practice as better than another. Should you choose to go practice a certain spiritual lineage or style, enjoy it. Should you be like me and not have a dedicated style as you see truth in everything, enjoy it. But what I would encourage you to do is this.

Believe nothing. Question everything. Experience things for yourself. Interact with life. Pay attention to cause and effect. Open your mind. Open your heart. Learn how to be happy for no reason at all with absolutely nothing. Follow life itself. Trust it. But keep a high level of discernment. Keep your mind out of things as much as possible.

Enjoy your existence.

SPECIAL THANKS

Special thanks goes out to some notable people. But it does not end there. There are so many people in life that have been instrumental in my development and they are too numerous to list.

CPSIA information can be obtained
at www.ICGtesting.com
Printed in the USA
LVHW050901300523
748311LV00009B/59